THE MAGIC OF BELIEVING FOR YOUNG PEOPLE

CLAUDE M. BRISTOL

Cover Design: J. Neuman

www.bnpublishing.net

info@bnpublishing.net

For information regarding special discounts for bulk purchases,

please contact BN Publishing

sales@bnpublishing.net

CONTENTS

1. SUCCESS AND YOU

How I discovered mind power - Belief is a miracle worker - You can use this mind power - It worked for these people - This power can be a blessing-or a curse

2. MIND POWER EXPERIMENTS

You are sitting on a "thought" - You are what you think - You must strengthen your mind - Beware of other people's thoughts

3. WHAT DO YOU WANT?

Is it money? - Is it fame? - A career in sports? - Is it a scholarship? - Is it the arts? - Make up your mind- It works for everyday things, too - Got your first job yet? - Once you make it, don't stray - Can mind affect matter? - Thoughts are magnetic - What is vibration? - Try this experiment - Thought spreads like ripples in a pool

4. WHAT IS THE SUBCONSCIOUS?

No limits to its power - Learn my techniques - Even movie actresses use it - Mind power is very, very old - The power is mysterious - Trick your conscious mind - Try to solve this - Don't underrate the conscious mind -Some examples of reasoning

5. HOW TO MAKE DECISIONS

The source of power - A universal hookup - These powers increase with use - The subconscious preserves life - The subconscious commands life - The subconscious powers life - Be careful when using this power - First prepare yourself - Get rid of all your doubts - Don't be in a hurry - Follow those "unreasonable" urges - The subconscious is wise

6. YOU WANT TO BELIEVE? HERE'S HOW!

Truth must be the base - Japan's "fake" suicide fighter - The power of repeated suggestion - Look for "plus" values - Famous examples of suggestion - Fear thoughts bring failure - Influencing people - Watch every thought - Superstition at work - He talked to his trees

7. HOW TO FORM MENTAL PICTURES

Don't daydream - Concentration is essential - The subconscious in action -Picture-making isn't easy - He caught fishes with mental pictures - Try it this way

8. TRY THESE TECHNIQUES

Warning: keep your cards a secret - Give heed to that sudden impulse - Overcoming nervousness - Executives are just plain people - A new way to sell cheese - Seeing what's before you - My, you're looking well!

9. FEAR AND IMAGINATION

Some imagination! - "But that's silly," he said - Think-don't talk - Auto-suggestion helps - Use simple statements - Protect your subconscious - Hammer it home - Don't follow the leader - Have an Active Faith

10. SEEING IS BELIEVING

Follow the rules - So you're going to work - Then use your reminder cards -Through the looking glass - Facing troubles - Seeing yourself - Sell yourself your ideas - Sell your family - How to use the mirror technique - Stare your worries away - The eyes have it

11. YOUR MONEY PROBLEMS

Do your part - He "sold" himself to the landlord - First, an idea - Don't fool yourself - Your thoughts are showing - The answer might come at any time -A "hunch" is something different - You furnish the ambition - So far, so good

12. GETTING AHEAD

The promise of the future - Think big - Never stand still - Find a better way -Keep your word - Make friends-and be one - Be courteous - Forget about yourself - Lend a hand - Be a wide-awake - Easy does it - Books are tools -Where joy is found

13. THE WANDERING MIND

How ideas grow - Learn to package yourself - Who gets the attention? - Protect your emotions - How others affect you - Tackle your problems - Emotional ailments - Cure yourself

14. MASTER OF YOURSELF

Never neglect your gift - White magic - Your mind is yourself - Keep at it-the day will come - Happiness is a state of mind - A child's imagination - Your parents and you - Live your own life - Begin to use your power

Chapter 1: SUCCESS AND YOU

THERE IS POWER IN THE MIND, UNUSED POWER, power which you must learn to control and apply. If you do, you can ask whatever you will of life and get it.

Understand that I am saying this to those young men and women with the good sense to look beyond the present into the future. If you are satisfied with things as they are this book won't mean a thing to you. The *you* I am talking to is ambitious. I've been developing and proving - in my own life and in the lives of others - the principles I am setting forth in this volume. But its invincible truth was brought forcefully home to me again only a few months ago. I met the artist, Hutton Webster, in Tucson, Arizona, only a short time before the shocking accident which caused his death.

"What made you a painter?" I asked him.

"Something that happened to me in Chicago," he said, his vivid eyes shining, his mouth twitching at the comers in his provocative smile. "I wasn't more than five years old and my father, a university professor, had taken me with him on a trip. We came upon a sidewalk artist and I was entranced. I wouldn't leave. I watched him at work and cried when I was forcibly moved on. From that moment I knew that I was going to be a painter."

"When older people asked - as they always do - 'What are you going to be when you grow up?' I answered promptly, I'm going to be a painter."

"My persistence in this statement began to annoy my father. 'I'm going to be a painter' was my childish chant as I went about all my occupations. 'I'm going to be a painter,' I told myself throughout the course of my school days.

"Naturally my father wanted me to prepare for the teaching profession in which he was so successful. 'I'm going to be a painter,' I insisted. Not until I began to win prizes and various Foundations gave me awards which financed my studies were my parents convinced. Then they helped me in every way that they could."

Hutton Webster was a painter. His pictures are hung in the great galleries of our country. Honors continued to come to him. Then he was stricken with arthritis. Sent to Arizona, he was carried from the plane on a stretcher. He recovered to some extent. He was able to walk with the aid of two sticks. He carried a tall stool about with him against which he leaned, seeming to sit on it. He could feed himself with a specially made utensil. But he had to be dressed and undressed. He grew a beard since he could not shave himself. And his hands were too crippled and too stiff to manipulate a paintbrush.

But Hutton Webster was a painter. He taught himself to paint by holding the handle of the brush in his mouth.

There is power in the mind. You can ask whatever you will of life and get it.

How I discovered mind power

Let me tell you how I discovered the germ of this technique for using mind power that I am going to develop in this volume.

On my army classification card I was listed as a newspaperman and I had attended an army training school to qualify for a commission. But the whole course was discontinued just as we finished. As a result I was landed in France as a "casual" soldier, unattached to a regular company, and it was several weeks before my service record, necessary for my pay, caught up with me. The few dollars I had before sailing had been spent at the transport's canteen and I was without money to buy gum, candy, or cigarettes. I grew bitter. Every time I saw a man light a cigarette or chew a stick of gum I vowed that when I returned to civilian life *I would make a lot of money.* Not a very lofty ambition, I grant you and, looking back now, my reason seems childish. But at that time I saw that aim as the foremost one of my future civilian life; it became rooted so deep in me that it remained in the forefront of my mind for many years. From that moment the whole pattern of my life was altered.

It was August when I got home and I was in a great hurry to begin building that fortune I had decided upon. However I found that the forces I had unconsciously set in motion were already at work. The president of a club in which I had been active telephoned me and told me to get in touch with a prominent investment banker. I did, and embarked on a career which later led me to a vice-presidency.

In less than ten years I had a sizable fortune. During those years I had kept constantly before me the mental picture of wealth. Lots of people in moments of abstraction or while talking on the telephone engage in what is known as "doodling." My own doodling was always in the form of $$$$-$$$-$$$.

I have told you this little story to suggest the mechanics of this science, which I call *the magic of believing*. Concentrate on any legitimate end; you will find the principles you will learn in this book effective. I have proved it again and again. For instance, one afternoon in Honolulu I got a sudden impulse to leave for the mainland. I purchased the only remaining cabin on a ship and as I started up the gangplank I said to myself, "You've had wonderful luck so far on this trip, the least they can do for you is to give you a seat at the Captain's table."

And that's the place to which I was assigned.

Later I had the opportunity to ask the Captain why he had put me on his list, for I was a person of far less importance than many on that ship and I'm not one whose appearance does anything for him.

"Sometimes," he said, "as we go through life we get the idea instinctively to do this or that. I was sitting in the doorway of my cabin watching the passengers come aboard and as you came up the gangplank something told me to seat you at my table. I can't explain it."

Do you see what I mean? I was learning from my own experiences to believe in mind power. I was realizing that I had run across something which was *workable,* even if mysterious.

I had been born with a yearning to know the "why?" of everything. During my years as a newspaperman, and again as a businessman, I continued my search for answers. I read widely, literally thousands of books on modern psychology, metaphysics, ancient magic, philosophy.

As I continued to study, observe, and experiment I came to realize that there is one golden thread running through all psychic happenings that makes them work. And that thread can be named by a single word, BELIEF.

Belief is a miracle worker

Here's something that I saw for myself. I lived for a time in the southwest and I had working for me around the house and grounds an extraordinarily gifted Mexican. He had been the subject of what he called a "miracle" and, though I am not a particularly religious man, I cannot dispute his use of the word in the light of his experience. As a result of an accident he had become afflicted with partial paralysis, which made walking an extremely slow and painful process. He had been told at the hospital that nothing further could be done for him; that his trouble was something he would have to live with for the rest of his life.

Carlos didn't accept that. With his son - a boy - he started on the eight-mile journey to the Mission of San Xavier where "miracles" were known to have taken place. Passing motorists tried to give him a lift but he refused their offers. According to his understanding he must make the journey unaided and on foot. So slow was his progress that he was on that eight-mile stretch of road for two days. He and the boy slept at night on the ground beside their route.

He reached the Mission so exhausted that he had to crawl the final yards up the aisle to the altar on his hands and knees. He knelt there and prayed. Then he walked out of the church, completely healed. Afterwards he was able to work efficiently and actively. He replaced tiles that had blown from the roof, repaired masonry on the terrace, trimmed trees and shrubs.

An old Latin proverb says: "Believe that you have it, and you have it." *Belief,* I insist, is the motivating force.

Dr. Alexander Cannon, a distinguished British scientist and physician, has declared that while today a man cannot grow a new leg, he could if his mind had not rejected the possibility. He says that if the thought is accepted in the innermost depths of the unconscious mind, a man can grow a new leg as easily as the crab grows a new claw.

A neighbor came to me not too long ago to explain how his warts had happened to disappear. He had been a patient at a hospital and he heard a man saying to another convalescent: "So you would like to get rid of the warts on your hand. Let me count them and they'll go away."

"Count mine, too," said my neighbor.

The stranger did. Later, happening to look at his hands, my neighbor found that the warts were gone.

In an article appearing in the *Canadian Medical Association Journal* of 1945, Dr. Frederick Kaltz said: "In every country in the world magic procedures to cure warts have been known... It may be anything from covering the warts with spider-webs to burying toad eggs on a crossroad at the new moon. All these magic procedures are effective *if the patient believes in them."*

Great investigators and thinkers of the world today, including many famous scientists, are discussing and experimenting with the subject of thought power. Charles F. Steinmetz, the genius of electricity, wrote: "The most important advance in the next fifty years will be in the realm of the spiritual." Dr. Robert Gault, Professor of Psychology at Northwestern University, was credited with the statement: "We are at the threshold of our knowledge of the latent psychic powers of man."

You can use this mind power

As my faith in mind power increased and my experiments in its use in my life developed, I began to teach the theory to others. I knew I had run across something that was workable. And I am convinced that any intelligent young person who is sincere in his ambitions can reach his goal, no matter how lofty, through the use of mind power. I believe that if you look ahead and plan your future, making use of the techniques I am setting down in this book, you will win whatever it is that you have set before your eyes as your meaning of the word "success."

It worked for these people

I have known men double and quadruple their incomes by the use of mind power. Ashley C. Dixon, a name known to thousands of radio listeners in the Pacific Northwest, wrote me that with only $65 to his name and without a job he had set out to prove to himself the workability of this science. And he told me in detail how from that moment, "Forty-three years old, broke and needing food for my family, I have made one hundred thousand dollars."

Dorr Quayle, a disabled American war veteran, wrote me: "It was no easy matter at first to accept your ideas. I had been stricken with partial paralysis of my lower limbs, which made it necessary for me to use crutches. For one who had been active in the business world that forced inactivity was not easy to bear. Necessity forced me into practice of the principles explained by you.

"I started an insurance and public accounting business. Now I am making a good living and know that the formula will lead to the fullest success. When you have that knowing *inside* you, fear vanishes and the obstruction to a continued life of all good has been removed."

A woman author with whom I had discussed my theories wrote me: "That philosophy brought me to New York on no carfare; it sold my stuff to publishers while I was working at a lousy job for $30 a week and living on it. Eventually it took me to Europe and bought me silver foxes."

This power can be a blessing - or a curse

Here I must give you a warning: *never use this mind power for harmful or evil purposes.* Since the beginning of man there have been two great forces at work in the world - good and evil. Both are terrifically powerful. The basic principle by which both operate is that which we are studying in this book: *mind power.* Indeed, very often the use of this principle develops into something wider than individual effort and becomes *massed* mind power. You see the evil side of it in what we call mass psychology, mob rule.

But you see its power for good, for progress, in religious revivals, or in the surge of what was called "The New Learning" in the times of the Renaissance.

Study the lives of the great men and women of history and you will realize how great a force for good or evil we are unleashing when we develop in ourselves this method of attacking the problem of living. With the key to history that a mastery of the principles and techniques in this book will give you, you will be able to understand why evil appears at one time to have the upper hand, and why good is in control at another time. You will realize that mind power has built empires - and has destroyed them. History records facts; you must learn to interpret those facts. You must be able to perceive the dangers into which civilization so often stumbles, the seeming blind luck which now and again saves a nation from annihilation. You must come to a full realization that mind power controls your future, the future of your country - yes, and the future of the world.

Natural forces can destroy or bless. Floods bring disaster; yet it is water that makes the desert to "blossom like the rose." Fire can wipe out cities; but it also heats our houses and cooks our food. So with mind power. You can make it serve you and humanity. Or, by its misuse, you can destroy yourself. I cannot emphasize this too strongly. If you employ the power of the mind for harmful and evil purposes it will bring you down along with others in a great and cataclysmic ruin. You have seen it happen to a man like Hitler. You can look back into the past and name man after man who has brought disaster on himself and on all his undertakings.

These are not idle words; they are a solemn warning. You may choose to ignore them as not applying to you since you are not one of the world-shakers. But your own utter failure would be as serious to you as Hitler's was to him. The great forces of the world - of which mind power is the greatest - can bless, and they can curse. Choose the blessings. Go forward toward your goal, your ambition, with the conviction that it is good.

And I assure you that it is yours for the taking.

Chapter 2: MIND POWER EXPERIMENTS

IN ORDER TO GET A CLEARER UNDERSTANDING OF OUR subject we must give thought to *thought* itself.

No one knows what thought is, not really. We say that it is some sort of mental process; which means no more than saying thought is thought. But like electricity, it works. We even know how to make it work. We see signs of its presence and of its activities everywhere. Say you are driving along a broad thoroughfare. You think you are safe; you have right-of-way; you are keeping some distance between you and the car in front of you. Then a reckless driver comes around a comer on two wheels into that limited space. You see him, you think, and in response to your thinking you act. You flash a warning to the car behind you and you slow down just enough to avoid hitting him but not endangering the following cars. This takes quick mental and physical adjustment. Explain it? You can't.

Even more inexplicable is the "thinking" done by animals. Every dog lover knows that the mental processes of his pet are often evident. A friend of mine had an experience that left him completely convinced on that score. He went to call on a man whom he knew slightly. There was no response to his knock, so, finding the door unlocked, he entered the hall and haloed. No one answered.

The family collie greeted him and permitted himself to be patted. My friend decided to wait and seated himself in the living room. When nobody appeared after some ten or fifteen minutes he thought he might as well return later in the day. But the collie would not permit him to rise from his chair. The growl that greeted any offer of movement wasn't to be mistaken.

My friend stayed in that chair for two hours. The dog was friendly but on guard. His "thinking" was as evident as that of the driver of the car: you knew what it had been, judging by his actions.

You are sitting on a "thought"

What about the chair in which you are sitting? It was first a "thought" in the mind of the designer and then in the mind of the manufacturer before it became a chair for your use. What about the pane of glass through which you are looking? How did it come to replace the oiled paper of primitive days? Only as a result of thought, of experimentation, and more thought.

All the "things" which make up our lives - typewriters and houses, airplanes and ocean liners, thread, needles and pins - came into existence as thoughts before they became available for use. We see everywhere about us evidences of mental processes, even though we cannot explain them.

Ralph Waldo Emerson declared that the ancestor of every action is thought. That, again, is an idea worth thinking about. When we understand it and admit its truth, we begin to realize that our world is the result of creative thinking and is governed by thought.

Nothing exists, as we have said above, that did not have its counterpart first in some mind or succession of minds. Many centuries ago Buddha said: "All that we are is the result of what we have thought."

You are what you think

That brings the subject closer; makes it less a theory and more a matter of personal experience. *You are what you think.* Your flesh, bones, muscles can be reduced to 70 percent water and a few chemicals of small value. But your mind - what you think - has made you what you are.

You could not sit down in a chair until your mind told your muscles to go through the complicated process of putting you into your chair. You could not sit holding this book until your mind told your hand to do so. You get up in the morning, eat your breakfast, walk, drive a car only as a result of thought impulses. The motions you make may become more or less automatic, caused by physical reflexes, but behind every one of them is thought.

Do you question this? How does a football coach make a team out of eleven differently minded boys? He gets them in front of a blackboard, doesn't he? He trains their minds; then he sends them out on the field to get from their bodies what their minds tell them to do.

How do you learn to swim? Until your mind has been brought to understand what the body must do when in the water, you don't swim; you sink.

Carry this a step further. The way you walk, the way you stand, your manner of dress all reflect the way you think. A sloppy carriage often indicates sloppy thinking. An alert, upright body is a sign of inward self-confidence and strength.

What you exhibit outwardly you are inwardly. You are the product of your own thought. "As a man thinketh in his heart, so is he." What you believe yourself to be, that you are.

Thought is the original source of all wealth, all success, all gain - material or spiritual. Thought has preceded all great discoveries and inventions, all achievement. Without thought there would be no transcontinental rail and airlines, no intercommunication by telephone, telegraph, or cable, no - and think about this - no modern conveniences. We would still be living in caves and eating roots.

Whether you are a good student with a promising future, or a stumbling, bumbling clod of a boy or girl is entirely a matter of your own mental choice, your own use of the mind that is yours by right of birth.

I can't emphasize this too strongly. Your thoughts will make or break you. When you realize that no action, good or bad, comes unless it is first generated in the mind, it is easy to understand what the Bible meant when it said, "Whatsoever a man soweth, that shall he also reap." Your sowing is mental; your reaping without doubt will be in the external circumstances of your life.

Do you see what that means, what it can mean to you? It leads us to a conclusion that is almost too wide for our understanding.

You must strengthen your mind

If the mind has made us what we are, the mind can make us what we want to be. Maybe you don't believe me. I said the idea was too big to take in all at once.

But listen. History is filled with accounts of weak people made strong and also, we must admit, of strong people made weak.

You know the story of Florence Nightingale. She was not only weak but a woman, in a day when the words meant the same thing. Born to wealth and social position, she had, in the eyes of her family, one obligation, one destiny: to marry well.

As for the nursing profession, it was all but nonexistent. Yet she had a mind that saw a great need. The sick and the wounded needed nursing. She started by scrubbing the corridor floor at the Fliedner Nursing School in Germany and soon showed that she could not only scrub floors but bind wounds, and, with her encouraging talk, revive hope. During the Crimean War the men in the British War Office scoffed, but reluctantly let the "madcap" have her way.

She organized at her own expense a private expedition of nurses and took them to the battlefront. The officers in charge wanted no women to interfere with their work, but, under the leadership of this originator of modern nursing, the women took over the handling of the hospital. By her "thinking" she lifted the work of nursing into the realm of honor we recognize today.

What about the Bible story of Samson and Delilah? You don't believe, do you - I don't - that the cutting of his hair actually made Samson lose his great strength? That was only a symbol. He lost his power when he yielded his mind to the influence of an evil woman. He regained his strength - again symbolized by the growth of his hair - when he had freed his mind from the domination of her mind. And again his thoughts made him a mighty man, able to bring down ruin upon the wicked.

From the beginning of civilization the molding of men has been done by those who knew something of the great power of thought. Religious leaders, kings, warriors, statesmen have understood and used this science. Men of powerful, dynamic thought have led people into freedom, or into slavery. It is particularly important to us in this day when those two fates are struggling for predominance.

When those two ideas - one leading to slavery and the other to individual freedom - are at grips, it is essential that we study our own thoughts, try to understand them, learn how to use them, learn to draw upon this great source of power which lies within us.

Beware of other people's thoughts

We must also realize that many of our thoughts, our ideas, are not ours at all. Sometimes we are molded by the thoughts of others. Conversations that we hear, radio programs to which we listen, what we read in books and newspapers, what we see and hear in the theater or on television - all of these influences bombard us.

Sometimes they open our minds to deeper vision and understanding, but often they upset our thinking, weaken our self-confidence, turn us away from some high purpose we had in mind.

There was a time when I would have laughed at people who talked about the magnetic force of thought, how it can affect other people and even influence inanimate things at great distances. Not any more; I don't laugh at any claim to the power of thought, whether it is within my own experience, or beyond and outside it. I am open-minded on this subject. It is developing too fast and its implications reach into infinity. I am even willing to concede that thought might change the surface of the entire globe.

But we aren't dealing with those distant realms of thought; we are working with its powers within our own reach.

The famous Irish editor and poet, the late George Russell, has been quoted as saying that we become what we contemplate. We take that for our immediate field: we decide what we want to become, then we start to contemplate it.

Herbert D. Seibert wrote an article for the *Commercial and Financial Chronicle,* which he called "El Dorado." I should like to quote from it.

El Dorado, a country rich beyond all precedent... lies at every man's door. Your bonanza lies under your feet. Your luck is ready at hand. All is within; nothing is without, though it often appears that men...by dumb luck...strike bonanzas... Man individually and collectively is entitled to life in all abundance... "That they might have life and have it more abundantly" is the law. What do you seek?

Let each man seek the El Dorado within himself. Power is plentiful. The source is inexhaustible... It is not the power that is lacking; it is the will. When one finds oneself, the will becomes automatically set toward El Dorado.

The great physician, Paracelsus, said: "The human spirit is so great a thing that no man can express it; could we rightly comprehend the mind of man nothing would be impossible to us upon the earth. Through faith the imagination is invigorated and completed, for it really happens that every doubt mars its perfection. Faith must strengthen the imagination, for faith establishes the will."

"Man, know thyself," thine own individual self, is everlastingly the supreme command. Self-knowers always dwell in El Dorado; they drink from the fountain of youth, and are at all times owners of all they wish to enjoy.

Chapter 3: WHAT DO YOU WANT?

NOW THAT WE HAVE COME TO ADMIT THE PART thought plays in our lives, the next step is easy: *you must determine precisely what you want.*

Starting with a general idea that you want to be a success isn't enough. Your desire must be an all-absorbing one and all your energies must be concentrated and applied without let-up.

The world is filled with people who have worked hard but who have little to show for it. Something more than hard work is necessary. You must have an exact goal, and you must have a firm belief in your ability to reach it.

Is it money?

Every person has his own idea of what "success" means to him. What does it mean to you?

You may think that life will be completely satisfying if you can have a lot of money. You are not in the minority, if that is your aim. I have already confessed to my own early domination by that idea. If such is your considered ambition, you must make your aim specific.

How much is "a lot of money" to you? Settle upon the exact figures that would satisfy this aim. Draw your mental pattern clearly. See yourself possessing that amount of money; know the kind of life you would live. Be specific.

Is it fame?

Or is your idea of success a vague desire for fame? Do you want to stand out from your fellows, have a name that will mean something when mentioned? When name-droppers are around, do you want to have one of the names they will "drop"? You'll have to do some pretty definite and accurate thinking to make that ambition come true.

Fame is a wide-open word. You will have to choose your field of action. Science? Literature? Exploration? Narrow it down; make your picture of yourself definite. A vague desire for fame never got anybody anywhere. I'm sure Winston Churchill knew himself for a marked man from his earliest youth. Read his life. See for yourself how clear was his thinking, how definite and unswerving his aim.

THE MAGIC OF BELIEVING FOR YOUNG PEOPLE

What do you want from life; in what field do you wish to strive and accomplish? Your answers to those questions are the factors which will determine your whole life from now on.

A career in sports?

Perhaps you're a boy who has been a star in sandlot baseball and you want to go to the Big Leagues. All right. You can. But go to work at it. Keep the idea of major league baseball ever present in your mind. See yourself on the team you have chosen to join. Know what position you are going to play; mentally live the life, travel with the team, go through spring training. Never doubt; never question; never lose the picture. And meantime - play baseball; the best baseball you are capable of playing, learning, practicing, and believing.

Is it a scholarship?

Are your aims scholastic? If so, you know your subject, of course. But have you decided where you will go for your advanced degrees? Never mind if you haven't the money; set your mind to work. Be definite in your ambition; your thinking will bring it about.

Is it the arts?

Are you aiming at playing a leading role in some one of the arts? Is your gift a fine voice? Do you want an operatic career? See yourself there. All the years of training that are before you will fall into their proper niche - voice training, language study, coaching in the roles to which you aspire - if your mind, with its vision clear, is directing your preparatory activities.

Make up your mind

These methods of procedure will be equally true whether your aim is biology or baseball, travel or teaching. Your mind must take control and direct all your preliminary training if you are to arrive at that shining goal, "success." And while that is happening you must believe in and see in your mind your aim accomplished. You must carry always the mental picture of yourself at the top.

Here is something you will find hard to believe. Not one in a hundred of high school graduates - I'll broaden that and say not one in a hundred of college graduates - knows what he wants. He's gone through school. What next? He'll have to get some sort of job that will make him a living. What? Oh, anything. The work doesn't matter, so long as it pays well.

Are those young people going to get anywhere in life? You know they are not. They'll go around and around and end up nowhere. They don't know what they want: they aren't planning to get anywhere. And they won't. There's nothing in this book to help a drifter.

I am writing for the young man or young woman with ambition, one who means to get on in life, who aims at success. And I am deeply in earnest when I say that the first requirement is to sit down with yourself and chart your course.

Analyze yourself, examine your various interests and talents, settle with yourself which one to cultivate, make your aim specific. Know where you are going, set your heart on it, and I will help you to whatever degree of success you want.

It is vital that you know exactly what you want out of life. You must know where you are headed. Do I seem to be repeating myself? I am; and it's what you have to do yourself. Repeat and repeat to yourself what you want out of life, until the idea is unshakably fixed in your mind.

It works for everyday things, too

Do that with your ambitions. Think about them in the daytime, dream about them at night. Make that picture of your successful achievement so clear that it keeps coming up before your eyes without conscious cooperation on your part. That is Lesson One.

Am I making this too long-range? It is equally possible to use mind power in the smaller matters of daily living. Perhaps you are still in school and, to your shame, are a below-average student. You can do something about that. You can set your sights as high as you like. You can be among the first ten in your class if you learn to use mind power.

Or you may be a girl in that upper ten and unhappy because few or none of the boys you know think of you when it comes to dating. You can let mind power take care of that.

Or maybe you're a boy whose whole interest is in mechanics, and your father not only refuses to consider letting you have a car of your own even though you have earned the money to make that first down payment; indeed, he refuses to trust you with the family car. You can remedy that situation. But the way to remedy it is not by nagging and sulking but by mental pressure. See yourself behind the wheel of the car you have decided on buying; never lose that picture. You'll win.

Or you're in college and have gone out for football but you can't make the team. It is the thing you want above all others. If you want it, if you use mind power to get it, you will. It may take time, for your body will have to be trained to the skill that will earn you the position you see yourself filling. This isn't a hocus pocus science.

When you put your mind to work for you, you're like an ocean liner coming into harbor: you've taken on a pilot. You've surrendered guidance to him, you obey his commands, and he brings you in.

Got your first job yet?

Are you struggling in your first job and finding the going hard? You're an office filing clerk perhaps. And you're so nervous you can't put your hands on the papers you know you put under the correct headings. Your boss is impatient. You're all thumbs and your tongue sticks to the roof of your mouth. You want to keep this job, it is going to take you places if you can make good. All right; make good. And let your mind tell you how to do it. As soon as you have learned to see yourself as a success you will have taken that first long stride toward being a success.

I knew a girl - a college junior - whose head was full of dreams. She was going to be a poet; she would write verses about this and that and her school friends were impressed. But her instructor wasn't; she knew that the verses were not very original. Gently she turned the girl in a different direction and helped her fix her eyes on a career on the stage, for her acting talent was real.

Indeed, this girl might have had a degree of success in a number of different fields she was so gifted. But this teacher realized the need for concentration on one single, possible dream. And concentration won. As soon as she began seeing herself as an actress - only that, with no bypaths leading off into other pleasant occupations - she began to make progress. Yes, you'd know her name if I told you.

Once you make it, don't stray

But this story has a moral. Having reached her goal, she wasn't content. She didn't concentrate on being a better and better actress all the time. She let her mind stray; she followed this interest and that and she never went any higher in her profession than the point she had reached in the beginning. *Mind power can put you where you want to go and it can keep you there - but only if you are faithful in its use, obedient to its commands.*

And if you begin your study of the use of mind power with these lesser achievements, don't be satisfied. Move your goal ahead.

If you are the boy who wanted above all else to make the team when in school, let your next picture of yourself be that of captain of the team. If you want to make a profession of football, move your aim up; go after a coaching job in your mental approach.

If you're the poor student who wanted to be among the first ten, don't stop there. See yourself as scholarship material; see yourself winning scholastic honors. Where is this increased ability leading you? Do you see yourself in some profession? Look ahead. Plan. Set your heart on some achievement far ahead, and use the mind power you have been cultivating to get you there.

Imagine for yourself something that will compel you to seek new and greater abilities within yourself all the time. It is the desire for something new, for wider horizons, fresh resources that will change your life and draw from you the full expenditure of your gifts.

See this picture of yourself clearly and believe that it will come to pass. It is this *power of believing* alone that sets in motion those inner forces by which you add what I call *plus-values* to your life.

You begin with desire, if you ever mean to achieve more than you now have or are. It is the prime motivating force in all of us. Without an all-consuming desire nothing can be achieved. But there is more required of you than desire.

Can mind affect matter?

For centuries outstanding thinkers have claimed that man through his mind could shape events and control matter. The late A. Conan Doyle, creator of Sherlock Holmes, was for many years a member of the British Society for Psychical Research. He declared that there was a constructive and a destructive power in thought alone, which was akin to the "faith that can move mountains." He added that he believed man could actually separate the molecules of a solid object!

Materialists scoffed at this statement. But we are seeing today what is being done with radar and how radio waves go through wood, brick, steel and other so-called solid objects. If thought waves - or whatever they are - can be tuned to even higher frequencies, why can't they affect the molecules of solid objects?

Thoughts are magnetic

What does this mean to you? Why should you, a boy who is aiming at becoming an athletic coach, a girl who wants to be a successful actress, care about the effect of thought on solid objects?

Meditate on it for a few minutes. You have heard for years, I am sure, the statement that thought attracts that upon which it is directed. Have you read the Book of Job in the Bible? You should. For it was Job who said, "The thing which I greatly feared is come upon me." Our fear thoughts are just as magnetic in attracting troubles to us as our constructive and positive thoughts are in attracting the opposite. Thought does "create after its kind."

Go into the classroom to take an examination fearing that you will fail, and the chances are you will fail. You can be so afraid that you won't even be able to answer the questions which you know; you won't recognize them for what they are, because fear closes your mind.

Have you read Milton's *Comus?* The maiden, lost in the woods, taken prisoner by the evil spirits abroad there, could not be harmed by them, because she was unafraid. Men on the battlefield have died of fear, their bodies untouched by enemy fire.

Think about this. When the truth of it sinks into your consciousness you will give more attention to the kind of thoughts you permit yourself to think. And you will begin to realize the awe-inspiring power which is yours to use.

Let me go further, for this is a tremendous idea. Thoughts do create and exercise control far beyond any limits known to man. I cling to that theory. I have been an experimenter in that branch of electricity known as "high frequency," and I instinctively link this thought power with the phenomena of electricity. Such a comparison makes it easier for me to appreciate if not to explain the workings of the mind. Indeed the connection may be more than a figure of speech. Dr. Burr and his co-workers at Yale University reached the conclusion that an electrical atmosphere of their own making surrounds all living things. And we all know that mystics have always claimed the ability to see that "electric aura."

The ancient philosophers taught the theory of "vibration." Pythagoras, who lived in the sixth century BCE, held that everything that exists is vibration. The difference in the so-called solids is the difference in the composition of the vibrations. This may explain the claim of ancient alchemists that they could transmute silver into gold.

What is vibration?

We know that our nervous system is reached only through vibration. We say we "hear" a loud noise. The fact is that it comes to us by means of sound vibration. We "see" a green leaf; but it is merely a color vibration as gathered by the eyes and transmitted to the brain. If you are interested, talk to some of the modernists in the field of painting about "color."

Many vibrations are pitched at a much greater frequency than our five senses are attuned to: consequently we have no consciousness of them. Indeed, there is a dog whistle pitched so high that only a dog can hear it.

Do I seem to be wandering from the subject? I'm not. I'm asking you to follow the trend of investigation that has brought me to my own profound belief in thought power, for unless you can share that belief, you will be denied its use.

Let's consider another possible aspect of electricity. You have heard of the power of "the laying on of hands." Maybe you know how soothing to a headache can be a stroking of the temples by the hands of certain people. Couldn't this be some sort of electrical energy flowing from the fingers?

That very electrical atmosphere which Dr. Burr claims for each of us may enable us to cause certain impulses literally to pour forth from our fingers or from our minds - vibratory forces - that act upon others, or even upon inanimate objects.

If there is a form of electricity which emanates from our hands or fingers in particular, if there are waves - either dynamic or magnetic - caused by vibrations set up consciously or unconsciously by our thinking, do we not have an explanation of table-lifting, automatic writing, the performances of the planchette or Ouija board, and many of the mediumistic or occult operations?

Yale experimenters concluded that all living things are surrounded by an electrical atmosphere of their own making. Duke University, likewise, explored this field and proved to their own satisfaction that thought can affect material objects.

Try this experiment

1. Make a small disc of cardboard bearing the likeness of a clock face, with numbers from one to twelve.

2. Push a needle through the center of the disc.

3. On the point of the needle balance a sliver of cardboard shaped like an arrow.

4. Place the disc on top of a glass of water so that the lower part of the needle is submerged. (Make the disc just large enough to cover the top of the glass.)

5. Place your hands around glass, disc and arrow.

6. Bring all your concentration to bear and order the arrow to revolve, change position or stop at any specified number. (Have patience; results aren't always immediate.)

You may be amazed at what happens, although the success of this test varies with the mind power of the individual. Some people say the trick works by the heat of the hands, but can that explain why the arrow stops at the number you want?

Dr. Phillips Thomas, research engineer for the Westinghouse Electric Company, told a session of the American Electrical Institute: "We feel certain that whatever we do, say or think is accomplished by some type of radiation. We think such radiations are electricity."

Thought spreads like ripples in a pool

What do we mean by "thought radiation?" It is not unlike the effect of tossing a pebble into a pond. The series of ripples widen until they carry all the way to the shoreline. Connect this picture with your own mental impulses. The bigger the stone you throw into the pond, the wider the sweep of ripples. The more powerful the concentrated thought you start to work for you, the wider it spreads, the quicker its tempo, and the more rapidly will it do its creative work.

Creative force comes only when there is a fully developed mental picture, a rounded-out thought. When the imagination can visualize the fulfillment of an ambition, see a mind picture of your desire, then mind power goes to work.

Whether you are picturing for yourself a new dress, a television set, or a car of your own you must see it as clearly as if you already possessed it.

Chapter 4: WHAT IS THE SUBCONSCIOUS?

THE FAMOUS AUSTRIAN PSYCHOANALYST, Sigmund Freud, brought to the world's attention the hypothesis that there is a powerful force within us, an un-illuminated part of the mind - separate from the conscious mind - that is constantly at work, molding our thoughts, our feelings and our actions.

This division of our mental existence is called by some the superego, the subconscious, or the unconscious. It isn't an organ such as we know the brain to be. Science hasn't given it an exact position in the human body. Nevertheless it is there.

The ancients often referred to it as the "spirit." Paracelsus called it "the will." Or it has been referred to as "conscience," and "the still, small voice within." To many it is the manifestation of the soul, the Supreme Intelligence working within us, the voice of God. And men generally have come to accept the belief in a Universal Mind, embracing every living thing, all human as well as plant and animal life.

No limits to its power

For myself, I prefer the word *subconscious.* I recognize it as the essence of life, and the limits of its powers are unknown. It never sleeps. It warns us of impending danger. It often aids us to do the impossible. It guides and supports us in time of trouble and - properly employed - it performs so-called miracles.

What, *exactly,* is the subconscious? Nobody knows. There are only theories. But the subject is one which psychologists cannot ignore.

It's as fascinating to the scholar whose subject is the mind of man as the solar system is to the man whose interests center on the stars and the planets. We've even contrived - as our substitute for the astronomer's telescope - certain electrical laboratory devices that give us notable aid in our investigations. But the fact remains that we do not know for sure.

We do know that there is a faculty in every one of us, a mind that seems to work below the level of the conscious mind, which we can use to our advantage. We need to know how to tap it. We do seem to have the trick of feeding our problems into it, asking its attention, accepting its results.

It is not unlike the great machines that are being constructed in these days to calculate results from cards fed into them. The cards state the facts; the machine draws the conclusions. What an extraordinary advantage it is to everyone of us to possess his own calculating machine within his own person! How foolish we are if we do not learn to use it!

Gustave Geley, distinguished French psychologist and the author of *From the Unconscious to the Conscious,* wrote: "There is no artist, man of science, or writer of any distinction, however little disposed to self-analysis, who is not aware by personal experience of the unequalled importance of the subconscious." His conclusion was that the best results in life are obtained by close harmony between the conscious and the subconscious minds.

Up to the beginning of the nineteenth century the psychology of the subconscious was all but completely ignored. My own interest in the subject began when a professor I had in college referred me to a book called *The Law of Psychic Phenomena* by T. J. Hudson. After that I went on to other such books as they came from the press. Erna Ferrell Grabe and Paul C. Grabe wrote *The Sub-Conscious Speaks.* Theodore Clinton Foote gave us *The Source of Power,* and from Morton Prince, M.D., came *The Unconscious.*

There are many more recent books on the same subject but these are the ones that sparked my interest.

Learn my techniques first

What I want to do in this volume is to give you the methods, the techniques by which I have learned to harness and use my own subconscious mind to my personal advantage. As you pursue the subject you may find techniques that suit you better; you may even invent your own. But take my advice: don't discard any techniques that work for you. You're after results, not methods.

You will find, too, as you read on, some repetition. It is deliberate. Any subject so intangible as the study of the mind and its possibilities, of its quirks and processes, must be looked at from more than one angle. We must go over and over the ground. That is the only way in which we can clarify our own thinking, make the subject our own, and train ourselves in those practices which will make the subconscious serve us.

I am assuming that such a study as this is comparatively new to you. Hence we will take our time in developing our thesis and in applying its methods to the fulfillment of our own desires. A hurried reading won't do you any good. This is one of the books, as Francis Bacon said, to be chewed and digested.

Even movie actresses use it

Let me restate my main contention. There is dormant in every human being a faculty - whether it has been developed or not - which will enable him to succeed.

Stop there for a moment and let me quote from an interview in *Reach Magazine* of a young movie actress, Angela Lansbury, who believes her subconscious mind has been directly responsible for her success. "I don't mean anything magical or occult," she says. "But I think I've learned to tap the resources of the subconscious."

"How do you go about tapping your subconscious mind?" she was asked.

"Heavens," she said, "I don't want to sound stuffy or highbrow, but it's really awfully simple. If you tell yourself over and over again that there's no limit to the creative power within you, that's about all there is to it."

At least that seems to have worked for Angela Lansbury. That, and other techniques I am going to tell you about, will work for you.

You want to succeed, don't you? Perhaps your desires are small and immediate; or perhaps you are already burning with the wish to reach some distant goal. For either or both ambitions there is the definite chance of fulfillment. Believe that. Insist to yourself that you believe it. The more you tell yourself that you believe, the sooner will that all-compelling belief come to you. And you will have taken your first step toward achievement. For, insist the authors of *The Sub-Conscious Speaks,* the desire for success must be present in the conscious mind first.

Unless, in your conscious mind, you earnestly desire success in whatever aim you have placed before yourself, your subconscious mind cannot be put to work to bring it to you.

Mind power is very, very old

In reality, this mysterious faculty of the subconscious to take over and serve our conscious aims has always been known and recognized. Its strange and unusual powers are recorded in the sayings and deeds of men as far back as we have written history. Nevertheless, as I said at the beginning of this chapter, it wasn't until about a century and a half ago that psychologists made it the subject of special investigation and experimentation and called it the subconscious mind.

Ralph Waldo Emerson was certainly aware of the dual character of the human mental organization for he wrote in his *Journals:* "I find one state of mind does not remember or conceive of another state. Thus I have written within a twelve-month period verses *(Days)* which I do not remember the composition or correction of, and could not write the like today, and have only for proof of their being mine various external evidences, as the manuscript in which I find them, and the circumstances that I have sent copies of them to friends, etc. etc."

Today we use the words "conscious" and "subconscious mind" glibly, even if we have no clear understanding of what we mean by the distinction. We are more or less aware of possessing two kinds of mind: we endow each of them with separate and distinct attributes and powers. We believe each capable, under certain conditions, of independent action. There is no difficulty in comprehending that the conscious mind operates in the brain.

Cramming for an examination can, if too long pursued, bring on a headache. The application of ice to the temples can prove very soothing. Or if we have been doing some long-distance driving in a car, it is an admitted danger that the brain may demand sleep and cease to perform if pushed too far.

Have you ever watched chess players? After a degree of concentration that admittedly few games demand you may see one or the other of them close his eyes, put his hand to his forehead. He wants rest in the spot where he feels he needs it.

Suppose you are a football coach. You have given your brain a difficult problem to solve for you need some new strategy to use against a team already familiar with all your plays. In fact you have taken your problem to bed with you: you lie sleepless, your conscious mind too busy to let you rest. Finally you are so exhausted that you give up; you let it all go; you permit sleep to come.

It is then that your subconscious mind with its faculties which you do not understand comes to your aid. The moment your conscious mind lets go, that problem of yours begins to move downward. When the tension relaxes and you fall asleep, your subconscious mind takes over. In all probability you will wake up in the morning with the problem solved. Every player's part in the new strategy will be distinct and blueprinted in your mind. Your blackboard study is there, ready for you to chalk up before the team. Your mental picture is clear. Your part then is to interpret in action what your subconscious mind has worked out for you in thought.

The power is mysterious

Where did those thoughts go when your conscious mind released them? Where does that power reside that takes over when you fall asleep or when you deliberately give over to it something which your conscious mind wants accomplished? All we know is that it is there, somewhere, because of the results accomplished, the solved problem when you wake in the morning, the fulfillment of the commands given it by your conscious mind. Somehow it solves our problems for us.

It need not be a matter of sleep and waking. We can commit to the care of the subconscious a line of reasoning, an unsolved mystery, anything we want it to work on. We can do this at any time. The answer may not come for days. Then, suddenly, it is there in the conscious mind, fed upwards from wherever the subconscious resides.

Any writer will tell you how true that is. So will public speakers, composers, inventors, designers - any creative worker. If he is successful it is because he has learned the trick of feeding the problems of his conscious mind into his subconscious. He may not know that he is doing this; he may simply say to himself, "I'd better let this matter rest awhile. I'll come back to it later." He does let it rest - at least his conscious mind lets it rest - and his subconscious mind goes to work on it, solves it, and returns it to him. But very often he knows exactly what he is doing.

Louis Bromfield, the American novelist who died recently, is quoted as saying, "One of the most helpful discoveries I made long ago in common with some other writers is that there is a part of the mind, which the psychologists call the 'subconscious,' that works while you are sleeping or even while you are relaxing or engaged in some other task far removed from writing."

Trick your conscious mind

What Louis Bromfield does not say is that one aid to taking a job away from the conscious and turning it over to the subconscious mind is to go about some physical task. Take a walk, observing what you see; work in your garden, giving your attention to that occupation. In other words, take your conscious mind off the problem. Trick it into preoccupation with other matters.

Louis Bromfield continues: "I have found it possible to train this part of my mind to do a pretty organized job. Very often I have awakened in the morning to find a problem of technique, or plot, or character, which had long been troubling me, completely solved while I had been sleeping."

He then goes off into that fascinating field of speculation as to what the subconscious mind is, whence it comes, how reliable is it. He writes: "The judgment of the 'subconscious mind,' which represents inherited instincts and the accumulation of experience, is virtually infallible, and I would always trust its decisions over any judgment arrived at through a long and reasonable process of conscious thinking."

Personally, I go along with Mr. Bromfield in his theory that inherited instincts and the accumulation of experience lie in the realm of the subconscious. But I go a long way further in my theories of the origin of its powers, as you will see as this book develops.

Try to solve this

Here's an experiment, if you would like to try it out for yourself and don't do it with the idea that it is just an amusing parlor game. Take it as a possible glimpse into a science of which you are only beginning to become aware.

Three of you take three strips of colored paper: the colors should be vivid, the strips about an inch wide and three inches long. One of you closes his eyes. A second holds the three strips fanwise, as you would hold a hand in a card game. The third touches one of the strips.

Then let the first one, the one with his eyes closed, name the strip touched. He must speak instantly; the decision must be spontaneous - using, you see, his subconscious mind to prompt him. If he delays, his decision will be no more than a three-to-one chance his conscious mind has taken.

Do this repeatedly and you will be surprised at how often the correct answer is given. With practice the results will be almost 100 percent, for the subconscious mind of the one will become more amenable to accepting hints from the subconscious minds of the other two. And the holder of the strips must be a person capable of maintaining unwavering concentration on the strip chosen and one with a strong belief that he can transmit the vision of color to the boy or girl who has his eyes hidden.

As I said in the beginning, this sort of thing is not a game to be played for the amusement of nonbelievers. You are taking part in a serious experiment: you want to convince yourself of the truth or falsity of this claim to the phenomena of thought transference.

I suppose every one of us has formed a sort of picture of the two minds: the conscious mind in the head above the line of consciousness, and the subconscious mind somewhere below. Any picture must allow for a pipeline, a means of communication between. It doesn't really matter whether you picture the subconscious mind as making its home in your heart, in your lungs, or floating loose in the general locality of your breastbone. The important thing is that you believe it is there; that its communication with the conscious mind is constant; that, like the heart, it never ceases to work.

We know that that heartbeat can be quickened or slowed down by our conscious volition. In somewhat the same way, your conscious mind can affect the workings of your subconscious mind.

So, as I said, it doesn't matter what your picture looks like so long as you have a picture; so long as you believe in the existence of your subconscious mind and in the ability of your conscious mind to make use of it, to reach it at will. That we must believe if it is to serve us in accordance with our own ambitions.

Don't underrate the conscious mind

For it is the conscious mind that is the source of thought.

The conscious mind gives us our awareness of the events of our normal, waking hours. The knowledge that we are ourselves, here and now; the recognition and understanding of our environment; the power to rule over our mental faculties, to recall the events of our past life, to comprehend our emotions and their significance. These are the functions of the conscious mind.

More concretely, the conscious mind enables us to understand the objects and people about us, our own successes or shortcomings, the validity of an argument, the beauty of a work of art. In emphasizing the importance of the subconscious mind we must not neglect to give appreciation to the conscious mind.

The chief powers of the conscious mind are reason, logic, form, judgment, calculation, conscience, and the moral sense. You may not agree with that list; I'm offering it only as my own idea of what I ask and expect from my conscious mind. You may feel that conscience is within the province of the subconscious; that the promptings of your moral sense come up from the depths and are not always present in the conscious mind. I won't dispute that. Indeed the interrelation of the conscious and the subconscious, their constant interchange of subject matter make it impossible to say one functions exclusively on this line, the other on that line.

Nevertheless, there are certain mental attributes of the conscious mind with which we are most frequently occupied. By our conscious mind we become aware of the world about us, the objective world. And the means we use to bring to us that awareness are the five senses. Our conscious mind is the outgrowth of our physical necessities and is our guide in the struggle with our material environment.

Its highest function is that of reasoning, and by all methods - inductive and deductive, or analytic and synthetic.

Some examples of reasoning

For example: some member of your family is subject to occasional food poisoning and refuses to be bothered with medical analyses. What do you do? You put your powers of inductive reasoning to work. You watch what she eats, how much and how often. If you are patient, in time you discover that the rash from which she suffers is the result of eating strawberries. Your reason has brought you to that conclusion. You have collected facts presented to you by your sense perceptions. You have compared those facts by the mental process of noting their similarities and their dissimilarities.

In the end you made for yourself a generalized law: your sister should not eat strawberries.

Or you are writing a college thesis on which your grade for the whole term's work depends. You've been given a subject by your English instructor: for example, *What Kind of Man Was Chaucer?* You will be expected to deduce his personal traits from his writings, and you will have to prove your points by quotations. For this job you will call upon your conscious mind for its powers of analysis, of careful and detailed observation. You'll need more than concentrated reading for such a paper. You'll need the ability to draw closely reasoned conclusions. This task will be performed by your conscious mind doing a job you have given it to do.

Take the problems of your everyday life. Are you one who puts on weight easily? You give your conscious mind the job of watching your diet: of saying "no" to that particularly rich fudge cake you crave, of eating vegetables without sauces or any other flavoring than salt.

Do you have trouble making your allowance stretch to cover the items your father lists as your responsibilities when he decides upon the sum you will need, weekly or monthly? That, definitely, is a problem for your conscious mind.

If you are a girl who thinks she must have a new formal, you'd better not consider that cashmere sweater.

If you are a boy with a pocket all but empty, you'd better avoid trying to date an expensive girl and settle for one who will be content with a soda at the drugstore.

Admittedly in this book I am trying to lead you to an understanding and use of your subconscious mind. But the subconscious won't do all our work for us. The conscious mind must carry its share of the load.

Chapter 5: HOW TO MAKE DECISIONS

IF YOUR CONSCIOUS MIND MULLS A PROBLEM OVER AND over without being able to come to a decision, the time has come to call the subconscious mind to your assistance.

Perhaps you are trying to decide between taking a job this summer to earn the money for next year's pocket expenses or taking a summer course in that subject you are weak in to make sure of graduation next spring.

Let your subconscious tell you which decision is the wiser.

Or are you out of school and ready for your first job? Perhaps there are two openings between which you are trying to decide. Consult your subconscious. Get together all the facts on each; file them in orderly arrangement in your conscious mind. Be sure they are all there, that you haven't done a sloppy job of analysis. Then put the decision off, don't mull the matter over in your conscious, reasoning mind. Give your subconscious time to act. You'll know when the moment of decision comes; you'll know without a shadow of doubt.

Perhaps you are going through a time of discouragement when everything you touch seems to go wrong. You are beginning to think you'll never amount to anything. Don't let yourself think such thoughts; don't give them time to root themselves in your mind; protect your subconscious from them. Only a strong and self-reliant subconscious can meet and conquer whatever occurrences are throwing you, can bring you through with head up, shoulders back, and victory singing in your blood. *Belief* is the key.

The source of power

For just as the conscious mind is the source of thought, so the subconscious is the source of power. The subconscious is one of the great realities. It is rooted in *instinct,* as Ernest Hemingway said. It is aware of your most elemental desires, more aware than your conscious mind. You can fool your conscious mind as to the kind of person you are, your motives and intentions.

Haven't you known people of whom you have said, "They're fooling themselves." Haven't you caught yourself explaining away something you have done of which you are ashamed, making yourself look better than you are? "Rationalizing," the psychologists call the process. Yes, you can fool your conscious mind but you can't fool your subconscious.

Every one of your spontaneous impressions is down there in your subconscious. You look at a sunset and enjoy it. Your subconscious took in that reaction and preserved it. Some day when you want and need it, your subconscious - which is always pressing upward into your conscious existence - will give it back to you.

You meet a man whom you like or you don't like, you trust or you don't trust. Your subconscious will help you there. It may prompt you to look more carefully, to correct your first impression. Or it may warn you to be wary.

Your subconscious is a memory vault in which are kept records of facts and experiences which your conscious mind has sent below from time to time. It will keep them safe and will give them back to you at some future time when you need them.

But this subconscious mind is more than a great storehouse of ever-ready material to be placed at the disposal of the conscious mind. It is a powerhouse of energy. It can recharge you when you are exhausted. It can renew your courage when you are afraid. It can increase your physical and your moral strength. It can restore your faith in yourself.

A universal hookup

Here's something else: we must think of the subconscious mind not only as belonging to us, living somehow within our physical being, but also as beyond space and time. Fundamentally it is a powerful sending and receiving station with a universal hookup.

Through the subconscious mind we can communicate with the physical, the mental, and - according to some investigators - with the spirit worlds. Theorists carry this still further: they say we can communicate with the worlds of the past, the present and the future. Such are the powers claimed for the subconscious mind. They may all be true. It may have even deeper powers than these. All we know is that the power is there to do everything we have ever asked of it.

We believe *it has far greater power than we have asked of it.* As our conception of and our belief in its powers grow, so will our achievements. We have only to choose the pattern which we wish for our lives, and believe. Here is my credo: the subconscious embodies the wisdom of the past, the awareness and knowledge of the present, the thought and vision of the future.

Emerson called this power "instinct." But in his writings he endowed it with so many superior attributes that he must have been conceiving of "instinct" as that which we are calling the subconscious.

He wrote: "All true wisdom of thought and action comes of deference to this instinct, patience with its delays. To make practical use of this instinct in every part of life constitutes true wisdom, and we must form the habit of preferring in all cases its guidance, which is given as it is used."

These powers increase with use

As I have been saying, the power of this "instinct" increases with use. No one yet has struck bottom. The more we ask, the more we receive. (That sounds Biblical, doesn't it?)

Among its attributes I have listed intuition, emotion, certitude, inspiration, suggestion, deduction, imagination, organization, and, of course, memory and dynamic energy. Your own list will come to include these and, possibly, you will discover and add others. Each of us will always be adding to the list as our perception increases, as we learn to use the subconscious mind more and more.

Here's a faculty which has always seemed astonishing to me. It - the subconscious mind - seems to take cognizance of your environment by means independent of your physical senses. At any rate, you will find it knows things you had not noticed and so had not, by means of your senses speaking to your conscious mind, fed into it.

It knows more than we are conscious of knowing about the environment in which we live. And, notice this, it operates most successfully and performs its highest function when the conscious mind is inactive.

All writers - particularly the imaginative ones, the story-telling variety - depend on this faculty. They will give an accurate picture of an environment to which they have been exposed but of which they were not at the time consciously aware. You can test this for yourself.

Have you ever passed a house without especially noticing it only to have a complete and detailed picture of it come before your eyes later?

Have you ever sat before a telephone dial, needing a number you have not memorized, and had your fingers find their way by themselves?

The subconscious mind works when the conscious mind gives up. It works when you are waking or when you are sleeping. Somehow it seems to be an independent entity with a unique mental organization of its own; powers and functions that are distinct from our conscious awareness. It sustains an existence closely allied to our physical bodies yet operating independently. This is a conception which any reasoning mind finds difficult to accept. Yet this is a theory arrived at only by reason: these powers are deduced from the things which we know to have happened and can account for only on the basis of such independence.

The subconscious preserves life

As a result of my experiences I have built up these theories. I am assuming that the subconscious mind has the following three primary functions. First, with its intuitive understanding of bodily needs, it maintains and preserves -unaided by the conscious mind - the well being, indeed the very life of the body. More than you or I have ever realized, good health is in the hands of the subconscious.

You may not want it to take over: you may resist its natural functioning.

But the subconscious mind can and does - if not actively interfered with by the conscious mind - keep you well.

The subconscious commands life

The second function of the subconscious mind is to come to your aid in times of emergency. It springs into immediate action, takes supreme command independently of the conscious mind. It acts with incredible certitude, rapidity, and accuracy. By this faculty it often saves your life.

Say you are a woodsman and a mountain lion comes upon you while you are asleep. What saves you from jumping to your feet when you are awakened by the animal sniffing up and down your body? Your subconscious mind. It knows that you are in danger only if you move. The same instinct makes animals "freeze" in time of danger. The hunter can't see the deer until it moves. So the deer doesn't move.

The subconscious powers life

The third quality of the subconscious to which I wish to call your attention is its power to operate in a world where psychic forces are manifest. This is an all but untapped source of power to us. And since we don't know anything about the possibilities of this reaching out into the subconscious world of other minds, we do well to assume that this power is unlimited. For as we learn to trust it, to use it, we find that our own lives grow and broaden.

Such psychic phenomena as telepathy and clairvoyance have been proved to the satisfaction of many scientists. How much farther these powers can reach we have no idea; but we do well to trust them and to believe in them.

Indeed it is probably these very psychic possibilities that the conscious mind is calling upon, relying on, when it summons the subconscious to solve some vital problem. It is by its psychic activity that the subconscious mind brings to you from the outside events that fulfill your deepest desires.

And it is largely this third function that is the subject matter of this book. It is to the psychic touch of the subconscious that we must look for those events, outside the usual course of daily living, that bring success. And I am going to devote my attention almost exclusively to teaching you the techniques by which you can attain a more than normal way of life.

My explanations of the phenomena may be primitive. Future scholars will doubtless laugh at our naivete. But I'm not a scholar: I'm a businessman. My interest in the subject is in its practical application to my needs. And it is because I have found its use successful, the results verifiable that I am giving its techniques to you.

Be careful when using this power

What you want, I assume, is to learn the uses of the subconscious, how to make it operate to your advantage. Let me caution you: in order to draw upon the resources of the subconscious and awaken it to action, you must be very sure to ask it for something that is rightfully yours.

If, for example, you want a job that already belongs to someone else who is performing the details of that job successfully, that would not be a legitimate aim, you would not deserve success. Your subconscious might even balk and punish you: remember I warned you that it often works on its own. The initiative is not always yours. There are legitimate desires; be sure yours is one of them.

Selfishness will be no more successful when you are dealing with your own subconscious mind than it is when you are dealing with other people. Selfishness is self-defeating.

First prepare yourself

Examine your wish with all the ability of your conscious mind. Assure yourself that the aim on which you have set your heart is something to which you have a right, something you are capable of handling.

It won't do you any good to ask your subconscious for a role in the Metropolitan Opera Company if you are not already possessed of a trained, outstanding voice and have studied operatic music extensively. Be able and ready. You could, of course, take that aim as a long-range ambition, in which case the promptings and assistance of your subconscious mind would take the direction of preparation. And that would be valuable for in the event of your having your heart set on some distant goal, you do well to let your subconscious direct your journey. It will save you time and wasted effort.

Get rid of all your doubts

Having set before yourself a specific aim - whether near or distant - your next step must be to have faith, absolute faith. Theodore Simon Jouffroy, the French philosopher, said: "The subconscious mind will not take the trouble to work for those who do not *believe* in it." Indeed, in conveying your wish, your need, to your subconscious, you must go so far as to assume that the work *has already been done.*

Not only is it essential that you *think and feel* yourself successful in accomplishing your ambition, it is also important for you to go the one step further and actually *see* yourself as already in the spot to which you aspire.

Don't be in a hurry

There is then one final step: wait patiently. The subconscious has been given its task; its timing is its own. You can't know the series of events which must come to pass before your wish can be accomplished. Other people, other happenings may be involved. You must believe and you must have patience. When it is ready your subconscious will start the flow of ideas into your conscious mind, the plans, the course of action you must follow. You must be ready to accept its promptings, to perform as it directs.

Here is your program: you desire earnestly, you believe completely, you wait patiently. Then when the subconscious begins to direct your actions and to give you ideas, you must follow unquestioningly, unhesitatingly. That is part of your act of faith.

There must be no delay on your part, no reservation, no deliberation. You must be open to receive the message from the subconscious and, having received it, you must obey.

Act at once. Only by so doing will you succeed in making your subconscious serve you. Only by so doing can you assure yourself that it will continue to act for you when you call upon it. It is capricious I assure you; unless you believe in it, and back up your faith with action, it won't bother about you. You won't be able to stir the sleeping giant.

Follow those "unreasonable" urges

Of course your problem may not be one that can be solved in this manner. You may not be given a "blueprint," a complete program of action. Instead the whole proceedings may come to seem to you very involved and mysterious. You may have to trust to unreasoned promptings, you may feel an urge to do certain things that have no special significance, no logical connection with the accomplishment of your desire.

If what you most earnestly desire is a complete new outfit of clothes that you cannot afford and the prompting is to go to a party you had decided to avoid -go to the party. You will meet there, let us say, the person who will lead you to that outfit; possibly see in you a model for clothes which will be given you in payment. Things happen that way.

The subconscious is wise

When I say you must trust the subconscious I am laying out for you a program that is difficult for the conscious mind to accept, particularly if you are and have boasted of being a strictly logical person.

As I asked before, do you remember how you felt the first time you went into the water when you were learning to swim? You had to trust your instructor, to be sure. But more than all else, you had to learn to trust the power of the water to hold you up with only slight assistance from you. That trust isn't easy. Yet without it you would never learn to swim.

This trust isn't easy, either. Yet if you want the incalculable results I am promising you, you will have to teach yourself to believe in the power of the subconscious mind to do for you whatever you have entrusted to its keeping. And only to the extent that you are successful in establishing this relationship between your conscious and your subconscious mind will you win through to success.

You must continue to believe in the power and the wisdom of the subconscious.

You must perform obediently, with unswerving faith, those seemingly irrelevant tasks it gives you to do.

When you have done this, when you have once experienced the successful accomplishment of this whole program, then you will find your future relationship with your subconscious a matter that has ceased to need effort on your part; it will have become your habitual course of action.

You will believe; you will obey; you will be patient. And your life will be one continued progress from success to success.

Chapter 6: YOU WANT TO BELIEVE? HERE'S HOW!

ALL FORCES WHICH OPERATE WITHIN THE LIMITS OF THE law of suggestion are capable of producing phenomenal results.

Suggestion-auto-suggestion (your own) or hetero-suggestion (coming from the outside) - starts the machinery, causes the subconscious mind to begin its creative work. And right here affirmations and repetitions play their part.

It is the repetition of the same incantation, the same affirmation, the same chant that leads to belief. And once that belief becomes a conviction, things begin to happen.

You are just out of school; you want a job, a particular job. You've always wanted to be a newspaperman. You've sold papers on the corner; you've delivered them from door to door. Newsprint stirs your blood. Now you are ready for a self-sustaining role in the economic world. Your parents can't afford to send you to a school of journalism. You're going to have to learn your trade and get paid while you learn it. Tough. But it is the one thing in the world that you want. And, deep inside, you have the conviction that you can do it.

So great is your faith in your own ability that you walk into the building of the newspaper you have chosen to serve and up to the desk of the Managing Editor. And you ask him for a job. He looks at you, reads your eyes with the shrewdness such a man must have or he wouldn't be sitting behind that desk, and hires you.

You are starting your career in the environment of your choice. To be sure, you are only a copy boy and your pay isn't up to what you were making on your paper routes. But you're on your way and you'll climb. Of course you will. You'll be behind that Managing Editor's desk one day - when he's moved out and up.

Or you like outdoor work and you have apprenticed yourself to a building contractor. (We don't talk of apprentices any more, but what else would you call it when you are hired to do something you don't know how to do?) This man has a contract to build a warehouse. And because you mean to learn everything there is to know about this trade you have chosen, you get him to allow you to look over his shoulder as he examines his blueprints. And because he feels the tide of your interest flowing, he explains to you what those lines and figures mean.

He's a young man: this is his first big job. He got it because he wanted it; he believed he could do it. He believed in himself with such intensity that he made the man who was spending the money on the job believe in him. You believe in him, too - that's why you follow him about so eagerly.

Truth must be the base

This is the identical force and the same mechanics that Hitler used in building up the German people into a force with which he was able to attack the world. If you don't believe me, read *Mein Kampf.* Rene Fauvel, a French psychologist, analyzing Hitler, explained that he had a remarkable understanding of the law of suggestion and of its different forms of application. With uncanny skill and masterly showmanship he mobilized every instrument of propaganda in his mighty campaign of suggestion. Hitler openly stated that the psychology of suggestion was a terrible weapon in the hands of anyone who knew how to use it. He made the Germans believe what he wanted them to believe. He started his campaign of terror with slogans, posters, massed flags, which he caused to appear throughout Germany. He had his picture shown everywhere.

"One Reich, one Folk, one Leader," became their chant. You heard it wherever a group gathered. "Today we own Germany, tomorrow the entire world," became the marching song of the German youths. Such slogans as "Germany has waited long enough," "Stand up, you are the aristocrats of the Third Reich," "Germany is behind Hitler to a man," bombarded the German citizens from billboards, sides of buildings, by radio and through the press. Every time they moved or spoke to one another, they came under the hypnotic belief that they were a superior race.

After this belief had been sufficiently strengthened, they started to try and prove it. It was the *falsity* of the ideas back of the propaganda that defeated Germany. The power of suggestion as a technique is very strong; but *it needs truth as the base on which it stands.*

Mussolini used the same law of suggestion. He wanted for Italy, and for himself as Italy's *Duce,* a place in the sun. So the slogans began to appear. "Believe, Obey, Fight." "Italy must have its place in the world." "We have some old scores and new scores to settle." These and similar ideas covered the walls of thousands of buildings, were dinned into Italian ears by press and radio just as were similar ideas in Germany.

Stalin, to stick by our modern examples of power-mad leaders, used the same science in his campaign to build Russia into what it is today. The Institute of Modern Hypnotism in November 1946 recognized that Joseph Stalin had been using the great power of repeated suggestion upon the Russian people in order to make them believe in their strength and power. They named him as one of the ten persons with the "most hypnotic eyes in the world," rating him as a "mass hypnotist."

The Japanese warlords used suggestion to make fanatical fighters of their people. From the day of their birth Japanese children were fed the suggestion that they were direct descendants of Heaven and destined to rule the world. They prayed it, chanted it, believed it. And here again is an example of false propaganda ending in disaster.

Japan's "fake" suicide fighter

Here is an interesting example of Japanese technique. Ever since the Russo-Japanese War they had immortalized Naval Warrant Officer Magoshichi Sugino, fabled as one of Japan's early suicide fighters. Thousands of statues were erected to his memory. In repeated song and story young Nipponese were taught to believe that they could die in no more heroic a manner than that of Sugino, the suicide fighter. They believed this and during the war thousands of them gladly died that way.

Yet, ironically, Sugino had not died. He was supposed to have perished while scuttling a ship to bottle up the Russian fleet at Port Arthur, but he had been picked up by a Chinese boat. When he learned that he was being lauded by his people he decided to remain obscure and became an exile in Manchuria. Associated Press dispatches from Tokyo in November 1946 tell how he was discovered after all those years and was being returned home. But the legend had done its work. This terrible, persistent, deeply rooted belief, based entirely on fable, had caused Japanese flyers to commit that particular kind of suicide during the war.

The power of repeated suggestion

I've come to the conclusion as a result of studying various mystical cults and their teachings that they all have in common a basic way of operating and that is "repetition." Their followers are given words, formulas, or even plain mumbo-jumbo to repeat. The rigmaroles in many children's games are in reality left over, magic-inducing phrases out of our racial past.

William Seabrook has quoted examples in his study of the accomplishments of the high priests of Voodoo, the invokers of Black Magic. Our southern Negroes put a "hex" on persons who have annoyed them, often with uncanny results. Doubtless the witch persecutions of our own colonial days resulted from a real belief on the part of the so-called witches in their own power to "hex" others. We find constant records of the chants and incantations used by all the above practitioners of the various forms of the Black Art.

This principle of repetition is also used legitimately. There is White Magic as well as Black Magic. And we need not condemn a technique because it has been used for evil; it is also available for good.

Many religious faiths teach their followers to bring the desired results by the use of repetitious phrases. Buddhists and Moslems use set prayers at regular times of day. This principle can be seen in the methods of the Theosophists and the followers of Unity and other New Thought cults. Coueism made use of it. It is the principle at work in the beating of the tomtoms or kettledrums by savages in all parts of the globe; such sound vibrations arouse similar vibrations in the psychic natures of the primitive followers. They may thus be stimulated, excited, emotionalized to the point where they are ready to defy death.

Many of us have witnessed on their reservations the dances of the American Indians with their rhythmic physical movements. Many of them still practice their tribal ceremonies to bring rain. Then there are the whirling dervishes -surely an example of the power believed to reside in repetitious movement. Our own military bands of former war days stirred the emotions with their regular beat. Today many factory superintendents believe that music speeds up the timing of workers at the machines. And what of the old sea chanty? It was sung to get rhythm into the movements of sailors.

The power of repetition has always been appreciated and used by mankind even when not understood. Theos Bernard in his book, *Penthouse of the Gods,* brought out some interesting facts as to the repetition of certain mystical chants and prayers.

He claimed that he was the first white person to enter the city of Lhasa in Tibet, high in the Himalaya Mountains, where thousands of lamas dwell in monasteries - followers of Buddha. But that region is not so mysterious now, since the visit there in 1949 of Lowell Thomas and his son, Lowell Thomas II, who lectured on the pictures they brought out all over the country. Red China, too, has destroyed something of the kingdom's isolation.

Theos Bernard's book emphasizes the almost continuous devotion of these lamas, exemplifying this principle of repetition in their mystical chants and in their use of prayer wheels. He declared that in one temple monks spent the entire day repeating prayers they had started at daybreak, the exact number of repetitions being 108,000. And as these lamas accompanied him from place to place they repeated certain fixed chants for the purpose of giving him additional strength.

The subtle force of repeated suggestion often overcomes our reason. We use it in our American advertising campaigns constantly. Repetition drives the phrases down into our subconscious. We find ourselves believing them and finally buying the product however little our conscious reason has approved the slogan. In recent years we have enjoyed a vitamin spree; millions buy them, so potent is the repeated suggestion of their value.

Look for "plus" values

You must always weigh the plus or minus value for you of the many repetitions to which you are subjected in your daily routine; they are not all good. Take some of our American sayings, for instance. Repetition has made them almost as familiar to us as our names. You'll find there is both truth and falsity in them.

"What you don't know won't hurt you." Is that true? Look at it. There are some interesting implications there for our present study. A sleepwalker will cross a narrow board high in the air in perfect safety. Wake him, and he'll tumble off. In other words, that is in modern parlance, safety comes from trusting the subconscious mind.

But it is just as clear that what you don't know in an examination *will* hurt you.

What about the saying, "Ignorance is bliss?" Is there truth in that? Think about it. The words have become so familiar that they have become almost meaningless. They say something, though not quite what they seem to say. Ignorant of what? If we mean ignorance of cruelty, selfishness, meanness, we'll agree that we are happier if we don't meet them.

To the person who believes in the goodness of others, those others more often than not are good, and the believer is happy in his belief. Yet this kind of bliss is not going to carry through the lifetime of anyone of us, and so it is as well to add the saying, "Knowledge is power."

The man who has knowledge is like the oak tree, so deeply rooted, so strong that it stands firm against gales. Such a man is not influenced by every crosscurrent of thought that attacks him. Too many people are like saplings, swaying with every breeze, growing ultimately in the direction the strongest winds bend them. One man is held firm by the power of his own thoughts; the other is at the mercy of the minds of those about him. He is moved by any suggestion that impinges upon his subconscious.

A person must learn to guard his thinking, to safeguard his subconscious.

He, himself, must supply the repetitions that are to be the controlling influences on his mind.

Famous examples of suggestion

These principles are as old as man himself. Read the thirtieth chapter of Genesis if you want another example of the successful use of this principle of suggestion. Jacob used it on cattle to increase the portion of the flocks he could claim for his own. And Jacob, incidentally, became very rich. Why not? If he knew the principle of suggestion, as apparently he did, I am sure he knew other principles for controlling his own destiny.

Joan of Arc, the Maid of Orleans, under the suggestive influences of the voices she heard, went forth to save France. She transmitted this faith in her mission to others, and led France to defeat the superior forces of the British at Orleans.

Faith is the key word; suggestion is only one of the instruments by which faith works. William James, father of modern psychology in America, declared that often our faith in advance of a doubtful undertaking is the only thing that can assure its successful conclusion.

"Man's faith," he says, "acts on the powers above him as a claim and creates its own verification." In other words, the thought - literally - is father to the fact.

The late Knute Rockne, famous coach at Notre Dame for so many years, knew the value of suggestion and used it repeatedly.

A story is told of him that at the end of the first half of a particularly grueling game his team was trailing badly. The nervous players in their dressing room awaited the arrival of Rockne. Finally the door opened and Rockne's head appeared in the opening. His eyes swept inquiringly over the squad.

"Oh, excuse me," he said. "I've made a mistake. I thought these were the quarters of the Notre Dame team."

The door shut and Rockne was gone. At first the team was puzzled. Then they were stung to fury. In the second half they went out and won the game.

The same team, but Rockne had succeeded in his effort to suggest to their subconscious minds the idea of winning instead of being pushed around. Indeed, all great coaches have used this same magic of suggestion to stir their teams to the emotional heights where they did the impossible. We've seen it happen repeatedly in big games. The underdog comes from behind and wins the game. Newspapermen, reporting on the game, use the phrase, "... played inspired football."

One coach met the crisis in such a game by playing over and over a phonograph record of one of Knute Rockne's most inspiring pep talks. Repetition, suggestion, made the difference. Any athletic coach knows that great games are won in the minds of their teams, not in their muscles. The muscles must be trained and ready; the conscious mind must be trained and deft. But the subconscious of each man on the team, the combined subconscious minds of all of them, win games.

I am quoting from a newspaper dispatch about the distinguished coach of a second-division-minded baseball team, a group whom he literally drove to the top of the American League that season by the power of repeated suggestion.

"Day after day, through the hot, hard grind," this newspaper writer said, "he preached the gospel of victory, impressed on the Tigers the 'continued thought' that the team which wins must go forward."

The same force is at work in the up-and-down behavior of the stock market. Unfavorable news depresses prices; favorable news raises them. The intrinsic values of the stocks are not changed. The change is in the thinking of the market operators, which is reflected in the minds of the holders. It is not a matter of what will actually happen but only of what security holders believe will happen that causes them to buy or sell.

All over the world the word "depression" can bring the same reaction in the minds of the people of the country involved. "Times are hard," people begin to say. "This isn't the moment for expansion. We'll cut our advertising budget; cut all spending. Business is falling off."

And business falls off. The minds of those who have something to sell are suggesting to the minds of those who need to buy that this is no time for expenditure. "Wait, keep your money. Get along without those new clothes, the book you want to read, the car you saw yesterday. Don't send your son to college; let him get a job and go to work. Keep your daughter at home; her mother can teach her to cook. She'll need to know how in the sort of world that's coming to us."

Fear thoughts bring failure

What happens? If enough people believe that nonsense, a genuine depression is developed out of what had been a slight recession. Prophecies of evil come true. It only needs the action of that kind of mass suggestion to put the business of a country into difficulties. Fear thoughts can bring failure to a firm that is financially solid. Unemployment follows. Money, always sensitive, ceases to circulate. Banks fail. Mass fear creates that of which it is afraid.

It is the same with war. A people can scare themselves into being attacked. There has never been a dictator, eager for world domination, who has not scared his people into attacking "the enemy" by constant pounding on their fears of being attacked. When the great mass of the peoples of the world stop being afraid, stop looking for and expecting wars and depressions, that will be the end of these evils. Nothing comes into our social and economic scheme unless we first create it with our emotionalized thinking.

Dr. Walter Dill Scott, former president of Northwestern University and eminent psychologist, told the whole story when he said: "Success or failure in business is caused more by mental attitudes than by mental capacities."

Human beings are human beings the world over; they are subject to the same emotions, the same influences, the same vibrations. A village, a city, a nation is merely a collection of individual human beings. And what that village, that city, that nation becomes is the result of what those human beings think and believe. That is an inescapable conclusion. Every person is the creator of himself and, to an extent, of his surroundings. He is the image of his own thinking and believing. King Solomon told us, many centuries ago, that "as a man thinketh in his heart, so is he." And I have a profound conviction that the term "heart" as used in both the Bible is what I mean when I say the "subconscious." We - King Solomon and I - are not talking here about what a man thinks with his conscious mind, but what he thinks deep in his heart, in his subconscious.

You are probably too young to remember the details of the panic created by Orson Wells on the night of October 20, 1938. He put on the radio the dramatization of a novel by H. G. Wells, *The War of the Worlds.* It was a story of the invasion of the earth by strange warriors from the planet Mars. People, as we have often been reminded, are like sheep and follow a leader. They don't think: they accept what they are told.

You know - everybody knows - that no radio program goes on the air without an explanation of what is being given to the public; it is not the business of radio to fool its listeners. But people tune in and don't listen. And this program let loose a mass panic in New Jersey. Literally millions of men, women and children rushed out-of-doors, half crazed by fright. They besieged the police stations. Telephone exchanges were blocked. Highways were clogged. For a few hours following the broadcast these millions of listeners actually believed that our country was being attacked by invaders from Mars. I only hope the Martians - if there are any such - never find out how vulnerable are the inhabitants of the United States to mass suggestion.

You've attended the school rallies that precede big games. Speeches, songs, yells - all of them are a calculated means of suggesting to the minds, the subconscious minds, of the players not only the will to win but the power to win.

Sales managers of big industrial associations employ this principle of getting results by the power of suggestion. Some of them have morning sales meetings for the staff, attacking the minds of those who do the direct selling, who are the liaison force between the firm and the customer. They appeal to the emotions, try to convince the below-level personality that even the difficult customer can be sold and the reluctant one be convinced. The sales force must be made to believe in themselves and in their own powers.

Great armies have always been vitalized by the methods of suggestion. The commands and formations, constantly repeated in close-order drill, develop in the subconscious minds of the soldiers the instant obedience that finally becomes instinctive. The movements of the bodies of the men become automatic. And this results in a self-confidence which is essential to active combat.

When your body has learned to do, of its own seeming volition, easily and well, what is expected of it, you become sure of yourself. You trust yourself to behave well in an emergency: and from that very trust comes the correct behavior.

Watch every thought

All of this leads to the conclusion that young people must be very careful of the habits they permit themselves to form. And every act of behavior is a step in the making of a habit: repeated, the act becomes more and more liable to lead to automatic repetition.

Don't fool yourself with the false argument: "This once won't matter. I know it isn't right and I won't do it again - but just this once..." That is weakness, a temptation that is dangerous. The necessity to form habits of goodness, honesty, chastity, generosity is more important than it seems in that moment of temptation.

When you come to appreciate and understand the characteristics of the subconscious, the way it seizes upon that act which "doesn't matter" and makes of it a club to beat you with, then you will be more cautious about those first steps into wrongdoing. You are under obligation to yourself to form a behavior pattern that will give your subconscious only such suggestions as you are willing to live with for the rest of your life.

You may have joined some sort of secret organization where the joining ceremony and ritual was made very impressive. You have felt it yourself with each new initiation you have witnessed. This isn't meaningless; it is the calculated formula by which the subconscious mind of the new member is reached, his loyalty enlisted, his sense of belonging deepened. We see this principle exemplified more significantly in the ritual of religious organizations. Membership in any church is always accompanied by some sort of solemn pattern. Any means that can be devised to hold the attention, reach the deep loyalties and devotion of the person joining, is legitimate. Some organizations use secret symbols, lighting effects and some special garb for those officiating. Music is used to create atmosphere. And all of it is to put the participants in the necessary emotional and receptive state.

This idea of the use of ritual, repetition, is as old as history. Mediums use it in their seances and crystal-gazing performances. The gypsy fortunetellers always have their "props." Without this induced atmosphere, which makes the conscious mind drowsy, we would not be so easily convinced.

We all have moments of longing for the mystical, the miraculous. But that longing would not be sufficient to bring conviction without these devices, which lull us into acquiescence.

These methods of awakening and stirring emotional interest as an approach to the reasoning mind are historic: they originated, I am convinced, far deeper in our racial past than recorded history and are consequently more powerful in their results.

Even though there are many who deride the ability of astrologers, fortunetellers, and the like, there are millions of people in the world, including present-day financiers, statesmen, actors, actresses and people in all walks of life, who believe in prophecies. And I have long held that it isn't so much what the prophets foretell as it is the reliance of the subjects upon the astrologer or soothsayer that has brought those events to pass. A suggestion in the form of a prophecy, planted by the seer in the subconscious mind of the consultant, went to work immediately to make it come true.

Superstition at work

Another mode of suggestion often used in the more primitive days and carrying over into our times with surprising frequency is the use of charms, talismans, amulets, good-luck pieces, four-leaf clovers, old horseshoes, and rabbit's feet. These trinkets by themselves are inanimate, harmless objects. But when people breathe life into them by their thinking, they have power. And that power which makes them effective comes only with believing. Let's go back into history for our examples. In the days of Alexander the Great an oracle proclaimed that whoever unloosened the Gordian knot would become the ruler of all Asia. Alexander, with one stroke of his sword, cut the knot. And he rose to tremendous heights of power as a result not only of his belief in himself but because of the mass belief induced by the oracle.

Napoleon, we are told, was given a star sapphire as a child with the prophecy that it would bring him luck and one day make him Emperor of France. And this prophecy, this inducement to his subconscious mind and to the subconscious minds of all those about him, carried him to that same goal. Supernormal belief made of him a superman.

A cracked or broken mirror isn't going to bring you bad luck unless you believe that it will. But as long as that belief is fertilized, nurtured, made a part of your inner self-empowered as it will be by a like belief in the minds of many of your acquaintances who know that you have broken that mirror -the mishap will bring you bad luck. *The subconscious mind always brings to reality, makes to happen, that which it is made to believe.*

Are you under the impression that only the simple and the superstitious are influenced by these bad-luck omens? There is a story that a very intelligent man, a presidential candidate, was defeated by a horseshoe nailed upside down over his barn door. The two prongs of the horseshoe should have pointed up to hold his luck; turned down, they let his luck slide out.

He talked to his trees

Here is something else. You've heard the expression, "She has a green thumb." It actually seems true that some people have a mind power that affects the plant life with which they have to do. They grow better vegetables, finer flowers, more flourishing trees and shrubs.

An old gardener of mine used to mutter some sort of ritualistic phrases when he was planting new trees or shrubs about my place. I asked him what he was mumbling about. He looked at me searchingly, trying to decide, I suppose, whether I could be trusted with such inner lore.

"I'm talking to them," he said. "Telling them they must live and bloom. It's something I learned when I was a boy in Switzerland. Anything that grows should have encouragement and I'm giving it to them."

Thousands of professional gardeners believe in this affinity between certain people and the plants they tend. There are farmers who will plant seeds only at certain times of the moon. Superstition? I'm not so sure; it may be practical mysticism.

A thrifty neighbor of mine, a man of intelligence and mature years, will have his hair cut only when the moon is waning (or waxing, I forget which). He maintains that his hair grows less rapidly if it is cut at that time and makes a once a month visit to the barber sufficient. I said he was thrifty.

There's a tribe of Indians in Canada who talk to their halibut and salmon lines, hooks and fishing gear before starting to fish. They believe that the fish won't bite unless they do. South Sea Islanders, I've been told, offer food to their tools and talk to them, beseeching them to get results. And large fishing fleets in every civilized country are sent forth only after prayer for their successful voyages and safe return. Is this so very different from the ship-launching ceremonies in which we engage today?

Faith is a powerful weapon to Christian and to savage. Do you think, at the time General MacArthur was forced to leave the Philippines, he had any doubt in his heart? When he said, "I shall return," he knew that it would be so. He never ceased to know it. With our Pacific fleet in ruins at Pearl Harbor, with the Japanese in control of most of the South Pacific, General MacArthur made his statement. It was a statement of confidence and belief. History saw its fulfillment.

Chapter 7: HOW TO FORM MENTAL PICTURES

WITHOUT QUESTION, HUMAN IMAGINATION - VISUALIZATION - is a factor in developing the magnetic forces of the subconscious mind.

What do you want, deeply, absorbingly, at this minute? Let us say that your deepest desire is to bake a perfect pie. A foolish wish? Not at all. If you have been trying to prove to a serious-minded young man that you are not so frivolous as he thinks, that pie is important. You have invited him to dinner. Your mother has agreed that you shall prepare the meal with no help from her. Being clever as well as understanding, she has chosen a menu that is well within your capabilities. And she has suggested ice cream for dessert. But you are stubborn; you are going all out in this effort to prove your domestic adequacy - and that means apple pie.

You've tried before and failed. Your mother's recipe is in your head but not in your fingers. This time you have to succeed; and I am here to tell you how to do it.

First, believe; know in your heart that you can make this perfect pie. Don't waver; insist to yourself with fervor that you can. Then paint a picture before your eyes. Let your imagination bring up, to float just above your mixing board, a vision of how that pie is going to look as it comes out of the oven. Never take your eyes from that picture. Your fingers will take care of themselves; they will make all the appropriate motions - for you have taught them that before. But this time their touch will be so light, so deft, that your dream pie will come true. I promise.

Don't daydream

But you must make a distinction between daydreaming and a true, mental picture, the proper use of the imagination to attain your desires. You're a young man who thinks piloting an airplane the greatest job in the world. You walk the streets, looking up at a jet zooming by, leaving its trail of white smoke in the air, and see yourself in that plane. Perhaps you are making a long, looping curve above the city, perhaps you are dipping low with a deafening roar - and this girl looks up with worship in her eyes... that is daydreaming. It won't help put you in that pilot's seat.

Undirected wishful thinking doesn't have the power to release latent forces. What I mean by employing your imagination properly is that you not only see yourself doing the thing you want to do, but you go about making that picture a reality. The dream of becoming an airplane pilot can come true if you set about gaining the training that leads to that end.

First you picture doing that which you wish to accomplish. Then, after you have seen yourself doing it in imagination, you go ahead and do it in reality. A magnifying glass, when properly focused, gathers the rays of the sun and concentrates them so that they burn a hole in a pile of dry leaves you have gathered and in which you wish to start a fire. But if you do not hold the glass steady, if you allow it to waver, a sufficient degree of heat to start a fire will not be forthcoming.

It is so with your mental picture. You won't get results unless you are able to see it, hold it, concentrate it. Daydreaming does none of these things; its picture wavers, shifts, and accomplishes nothing.

Concentration is essential

I have spoken of Dr. Emile Coue, the little French doctor who threw so much light on the power of suggestion. He declared that the imagination is a much stronger force than will power. When the two are in conflict, he said, imagination always wins.

Suppose you are a young husband who has reached the financial status of contemplating the building of your own home. You don't start out with a picture in your mind; you have first to gather your facts, so that the picture, when the time comes to make it, will be accurate in every detail. You and your wife talk endlessly.

She wants a large living room, a room in which a grand piano will sound well but will not dominate the other features, will not dwarf the fireplace or the couch. You want a room to which you can retire in comfort when that future day comes that the children are old enough to turn the whole house into a rumpus room. She wants a kitchen with access not only to a dining room but with a patio where outdoor meals can be served, where the children can play while she works and still be under her eye.

All these details, when they are more or less agreed upon, you take to your architect. And he opens your eyes to the fact that the position of your lot, its slope, its neighbors and views must change your picture.

But after your picture is clear in your mind, then look at it, let your imagination carry it and hold it. There will be money problems. Hold to your picture. The architect will want many changes that would alter that upon which you and your wife have decided.

Hold your picture. Never let it waver as your eyes bring it up in your mind. Your architect will find ways to give you what you see; your finances will adjust themselves to your needs. Concentration upon a mental picture releases powerful forces.

Or take some project less ambitious. You are planning a vacation trip with your college roommate. Talk it over, make your plans definite, then give it to your subconscious to work on.

If it's a fishing trip, see the stream in which you want to fish, picture yourself casting, landing your catch: see it and continue to see it. It will come about just as you have asked your imagination to give it to you.

Perhaps you are out of college and are in your first job. You're not happy: the work you are given to do is unimportant and uninteresting. You don't see any future in it. You can't ask your subconscious to deal with any such vague dissatisfaction as that. You have to use your conscious mind; it has its duties, too.

Think. Analyze your discontent. Perhaps you are just impatient and do not see the future that really is there if you work your way through the uninteresting preliminary details. If that is the case, fix your eyes on that future which you believe to be yours; see yourself in the position to which you aspire. Never take your eyes from that picture, even while you perform to the best of your ability these minor tasks that will lead you to the more important work.

But if, as often happens when you first go to work, you really are in a dead-end job, do a very deep and sincere job of thinking. Do what you did not do when you took this job: find out what you would like to do, what you can do now with your limited, untrained capabilities which will lead to a position that will be satisfying, give you opportunities to grow, make you happy. When your conscious mind has done its share of the work, then you can give the problem over into the keeping of the subconscious.

The conscious mind decides; the subconscious mind brings that to pass upon which your conscious mind has fixed. And your imagination is the means of communication. The picture which you paint, which your eyes see, which you hold constantly before you of yourself in the position to which you aspire - that picture is the means by which your conscious mind communicates with your subconscious and starts it to work.

Learn to paint and hold these mental pictures. Your subconscious mind will then take over. Trust it implicitly; believe that it will do what you are asking it to do. Know that it will come up with a plan that will bring you to the place you want to be. It will tell you the steps you must take to get you there; and you must obey. You must follow its promptings with complete faith.

The subconscious in action

Let me tell you a story. A friend of mine got the idea of building a boat. He didn't know how, but he believed that he could do it. So he went ahead. He read, he studied, he mastered - in so far as he could from blueprints and handbooks - the art of boat building.

Before he started he had a clear picture in his mind of the way his boat would look when he had finished it. In the course of construction he found that he needed an electric drill but this boat was costing him plenty, and was going to cost him more. An electric drill would use up about $75 of his reserve cash. Anyway, he would only need it for a few months; afterwards its presence in his tool shed would only be a space-wasting annoyance. He tried renting a drill; that wasn't economically sound since he could use it for only the few working hours of his evenings and early mornings.

"I got to thinking one night," he said to me, "that somewhere there was a drill for me. I saw it being placed in my hands. The more I thought about it, the clearer the picture became. I saw it. I was using it. Nothing happened for several days.

"Then one evening a friend who owned a sizable garage - a man I hadn't seen for a couple of years - came to see me. He, too, was interested in boats and he'd heard I was building one. He looked mine over and saw how I was floundering around with the heavy half-inch drill I was using. He asked me where I'd got it, and when I told him I'd rented it, he said, 'Come over to the shop tomorrow. I'll lend you a smaller one you can handle.' Needless to say I got it and kept it during all the period I was constructing the boat.

"A somewhat similar experience happened when I was cutting the ribs. I had a small jigsaw but it wouldn't cut three-quarter-inch lumber. Then I found myself wishing for a band saw. That thought led to a woodworking shop a few blocks from my house where the owner allowed me to use a band saw if I paid fifty cents an hour.

"However I found myself running to and from my home, first to fit the ribs, then to shape them. I was losing too much time in the process and I kept saying to myself that there must be an easier way and I began seeing myself with a band saw available in my own shop.

"The following Sunday another friend who had heard about my boat-building project came to see me. I told him how I was slowed down by that band saw difficulty and he said he'd just bought one and wouldn't be using it for some time because he had to get his shop fixed up first. In the meantime I was welcome to use it. He even delivered it to me that same day and I kept it for a number of months. I finished the boat."

Here's another story. A man wanted an extension ladder because he had planned to paint his own house in his spare time. "I found I could rent one," he said, "but they fixed time requirements I couldn't fit in with my own working hours. I don't know how many times I said to myself, 'You're going to find a ladder.' I saw myself on it, reaching those pesky gable comers. So of course I found it.

"One Memorial Day I was taking my Scotty for a walk and in the house that backed up against mine - our two gardens met, but there was a high hedge between - I noticed my neighbor up on an extension ladder, washing the walls of his house. I called to him and asked him where he got the ladder. He said he'd bought it when he purchased the house but hadn't had occasion to use it before.

"That same afternoon it was over the hedge and in my yard; I had the loan of it for several weeks. My picture of myself painting my own house had fulfilled itself just as I knew it would."

These stories could go on endlessly; here's another that occurs to me.

A young friend of mine wanted a garbage can of a certain size to fit into a comer of the house where it would be more or less out of sight. He visited stores, secondhand stores, junk shops; plenty of garbage cans but not of the size his wife wanted.

Then he noticed some workmen making repairs on a concrete building across from his home. They were using some waterproofing material from a can, which was exactly the size he had pictured for his garbage. He asked them what they would do with that can when they were through with it, explaining his needs and his wife's unreasonable demands upon him. They sympathized. They said the can would just be left behind, but they did better than that. The next day it was in his garage, not only emptied out but scrubbed. All husbands are brothers.

I had taken my car to a shop for repairs. "I believe I can fix it," said the owner.

"Belief is a great thing, isn't it?" I said, wondering just how serious he had been in his use of the word.

"You bet it is," he said with enthusiasm. "That's what I try to tell these dumb clucks working for me." And he grinned at a couple of boys who were making motions of window washing on my car.

"It's the greatest force in the world and I don't let anybody laugh when I say so."

This man wasn't much older than the boys working for him: a veteran who had been thrifty and bought himself a business.

"Have you had any personal experience in the workings of belief?" I asked him.

"Have I! Say, listen!" And he settled into his narrative, forgetting all about my car's disabilities. "After I left the Army - well, I wouldn't say I left, exactly - the truth is I was in the hospital with a broken back. I'm not saying anything against the Army medics - they're the best. But when they told me I was going to spend the rest of my life in a wheelchair, I wasn't taking it. How was I to make a living if I was a cripple? A phrase my mother had used over and over came to me: 'One just has to believe,' she'd said whenever anyone in the family was up against it. One day it came to me: I was going to be all right. I knew it. I could see myself walking without a limp, getting about like anybody else. I had a picture of myself well and strong, and I never lost it. O.K. Look at me. Watch me crawling under your car. Am I a cripple?"

"That's wonderful," I said when he was upright again.

"I'll tell you another," he said, letting his two "dumb clucks" service customers who wanted gas. "I got my own place pretty soon after I got out of service. And then I was burned out. That had me worried.

"I couldn't find another location that I thought was any good and I'd about decided to go to work for somebody else when one night I faced things again, just the way I had in the hospital. I had to believe. I had to see myself with my own place, in the kind of location I wanted. That thought went around with me all day; it went to bed with me that night. 'You'll find a location within the next two or three days,' I told myself. 'Faith's not let you down yet. It won't this time.' And I went off to sleep, easy in my mind.

"The next morning I went to see the painter where I'd left the car I'd saved from the fire and I told him what I was up against.

'That's funny,' he said. 'You can have this place. I've just bought a building in the next block and I'll rent you this.'

"So here I am," he finished. "On a main thoroughfare, with more business than I can handle." He grinned, looking at the cars lined up, waiting for his attention. "I'd better get back to work. You leave your car and come back in a couple of hours. I'll have it running right."

Don't fool yourself by saying all these stories are examples of coincidence. I'm telling you there is no such thing as coincidence. Mind, your subconscious mind, supplies all your needs if you trust it, give it the facts, wait for its promptings, and obey. Make pictures. Reiterate your needs. Have faith. That's your formula. The things we think materialize; intensified thought brings them to pass.

Picture-making isn't easy

"Men who are devoid of the power of spiritual perception," said Paracelsus, "are unable to recognize anything that cannot be seen externally."

It is fairly well established that the subconscious mind works as a result of images thrown upon its screen. But if there is something wrong with your "projection apparatus," if the image is blurred, inverted, or a total blank, then you will not get results. Don't blame the subconscious; blame yourself.

Artists, writers, inventors, composers - people with well-developed imaginations - have the ability to visualize, to make mental pictures almost at will. If you have not this ability you will need to cultivate it. It is important to be able to see in the mind's eye the situations or objects you desire to see in reality.

He caught fishes with mental pictures

I knew a fisherman who could sit in a boat and pull trout after trout out of the water while his companions, in the same boat, using the same bait or fly, and the same mechanical technique, would cast or drop their bait in the same place without result.

When I asked him about it he said: "I put the old magic on 'em. I'm down there where they are. I tell 'em to snap at that bait. It works. I know it'll work when I do it. It always does."

He had the power of making mental pictures; and he believed.

When I told this story to another fisherman he snapped: "Nonsense! Any good fisherman knows his stream, knows what bait to use, and he catches 'em if they are there." But he could not explain why this man hooked his fish while his companions in the boat did not.

This principle works in the country club, too. Take golf. I've played with a man who is the most amazing short-shot player on the Pacific Coast. With his mashie or mashie niblick, he can place the ball anywhere he wants to on the green with a dead stop, as close to or as far from the pin as he desires. In fact, he's usually down in one putt.

"How do you do it, George?" I asked.

"You've played handball and squash," he said. "You know what it means to place your shots on the front wall. Intuitively you place it high or low or so it will rebound to a sidewall or result in a kill or an extremely low ball. I learned placement years ago in tennis.

You have a sort of mental picture where you want the ball to land before you hit it with your racquet. (Or with your hand, if you're playing handball.)

"Now I'm using that same principle in golf. When I face the green and before I swing my club, I have an instant, mental picture of where I want the ball to land. When I putt I actually see the ball dropping into the hole. I don't mean that a proper stance, a knowledge of handling the clubs and all that, isn't vital. That comes first and must be mastered before you're ready to use this picturing trick. But a lot of golfers have all the technique down pat and still don't get results.

"It's true I spend many hours in practice, and so do they. But the one thing I do in addition is to see and know where the ball is going to land before my club hits it. There's a confidence or a belief in me that I can do it. And with a mashie or a mashie niblick I use a backspin that brings the ball to a dead stop when it lands."

Picturization, you see, isn't a substitution for the know-how that wins; it is an added power that makes winning sure. You're dubious?

All right. Here's a newspaper story written by that famous sports writer, the late Grantland Rice. It's about a golfer whose ball always landed where he wanted to place it: 300 yards down the fairway or - if it was a chip shot - within two or three feet of the cup.

"Golf to me," Rice quoted the man as saying, "is played with the head, mind or brain, whatever you want to call it. Of course there are fundamentals of stance, grip, swing; but I must have a clear mental picture of what I am doing before I play the shot. The mental picture takes care of the muscular reaction. If there is no mental picture, what happens is a mere guess. This kind of playing means almost endless concentration of thought if you are under pressure. And there is no thrill in the game unless you are under pressure."

If you read Gene Sarazen's book, *Golf Tips,* you'll find he has much to say about mental pictures, objectives, concentration, confidence. All golfers are familiar with the words, "mental hazards." They are, of course, bunkers, traps and water hazards. They put fear into the hearts of the players. One course where I played often had such a water hazard, a pond approximately fifty feet wide. The distance from the tee, spanning this pond, was only about a hundred and twenty yards, an easy shot for any average player.

One member of the club, a great baseball and football player, could never get over that water hazard. Invariably he put ball after ball into the pond, to the accompaniment of profanity on his part and laughter on ours.

One day I said to him: "I know the water fools you. Next time just blot it out of your mind. Make for yourself a mental picture from the tee to the green; don't see the water in between. Just see an easy shot before you."

He followed my suggestion and his next ball fell within inches of the pin and from that time on he never had any trouble.

I've watched many pool and billiard players and I am convinced that the skilled oncs influence the direction and fall of the balls by mind control. Why not? If it can work in golf, it certainly should work on a pool table.

Roy Chapman Andrews tells of a Texan in San Antonio who fired 14,500 shots at small blocks of wood, tossed into the air, without a single miss. Mr. Andrews emphasized the perfect timing; but without knowing the man I would guarantee that he was a practicer of mind power; he had visualization and complete confidence that he could do it. And I'd advise using the same magic on target practice or trap shooting.

Great baseball batters, expert forward passers, accurate drop-kickers - people in sports who need to put the ball where they want it to go - can increase their performance if they realize to the full their own powers of picture-making and belief. Practice, timing and all the rest of the technical equipment cannot be neglected. I am only saying: add to them thought magic.

Dr. Marcus Bach in his book, *They Have Found a Faith,* tells of bowling with Father Divine. Immediately he noticed that the Father was no bowler; it was evident in every movement of stance and delivery. Yet Father Divine made a strike on his first try, and was completely nonchalant about his success. As Dr. Bach tells it, he rubbed the soft palms of his hands together as if to say, "What do you expect when the Lord rolls one!"

Dr. Bach also speaks of an interview with Rickert Fillmore, manager of Unity City and son of one of the founders of the Unity movement. He had asked Mr. Fillmore if Unity could be made to apply to a real estate venture. Mr. Fillmore replied: "If it works at all, it works everywhere."

Try it this way

Do you want to convince yourself of this power by a simple experiment? Find some small stones or pebbles and stand some twenty-five to thirty feet away from a convenient tree or post and start throwing stones at it. If you are an average person most of the stones will fall wide of the mark.

Now stop; tell yourself that you can hit that objective. Make for yourself a clear, mental picture of that post stepping forward to meet your pebble, actually colliding with it in the exact spot you have chosen for your bull's-eye. You'll find yourself soon making a perfect score.

Don't say "Impossible!"

Try it.

Chapter 8: TRY THESE TECHNIQUES

SO LET'S GET DOWN TO THE MECHANICS.

Secure three or four cards: ordinary, business-size cards will do. Sit down some place where you can concentrate and not be interrupted. This is important.

Ask yourself what you desire above everything else. Look over all your immediate desires and select that which is deepest.

You may be ready to fix on some long-range ambition: you may want something very special at the moment. But settle the matter in your conscious mind.

Know definitely what it is on which you mean to concentrate all your efforts.

Of course if your desires are so vague that you want one thing today and something entirely different tomorrow don't bother with this method at all. It won't work for you.

If you are the kind of girl to whom an invitation to a certain dance is an all-consuming passion, then your subconscious mind, if properly approached, will bring you that invitation. But if you are a girl who wants to go to that dance today, but tomorrow thinks she'd rather go on a ski trip into the mountains, and the day after is all for a shopping spree in a distant city - again, I say these suggestions won't help you.

Until you have reached the point in your life where one outstanding desire crowds out all others you aren't ready to make use of the power of your mind to attain that ambition.

When you have decided upon the one thing that you wish for, when you are sure it is your uppermost desire, then you are ready to use the cards that are on your desk before you.

At the top of one card write a word picture of what you want.

Make it brief; one or two words should be sufficient. Don't be vague; be definite.

Let's suppose that you are a senior in high school and more than anything else in the world you want to go on to college. But you haven't kept your grades high enough to convince your father that you deserve four more years of self-denial on his part and self-indulgence on yours. You can't blame him. Really this ambition has only become clear to you very recently. You've been having fun and not looking ahead.

All right. You've decided now.

Write *college* on one of your cards. Put it behind the mirror in your purse where you will see it several times a day. I've said that repetition is important; this is to remind you. As you see other places about your room where another card could rest and bring you that message, write *college* on your other cards and bombard yourself with the idea: in your handkerchief case, as a bookmark in a textbook. Put a card saying *college* to you in your pajama pocket so that you'll feel it and fall asleep saying it to yourself. A boy can easily figure out the best places for his cards.

Warning: keep your cards a secret

One caution... don 't talk about this method with your close friends; not even with your mother.

Talk seems to dissipate the strength of the attack upon your subconscious mind.

If others are likely to see your cards, you can find some symbol to use that will not betray you: a hastily sketched picture, or initials, or the name of a friend who is already in college. You can find some device to suggest your desire to you many times a day.

You may have to keep up this process of continued concentration for weeks or months: so be very sure of your desire, and very sure that you can trust your own powers of belief and persistence.

Give heed to that sudden impulse

You will have to proceed with your program of conscious wishing without knowing just what your subconscious is doing to bring about your ambition. *But trust it.* Be ready to follow its promptings. It may tell you to study harder, get better grades. That, surely, would be one way to convince your father of the seriousness of your purpose. It would be one way to prove to yourself that this is a serious and not a passing idea.

You will need to believe in the worthwhileness of your aim, as well as in the power of your subconscious to bring it about. Perhaps your future will depend on this growing faith in yourself and your own latent ability. Your subconscious will prompt you to other ways of bringing about your opportunity for further education.

You will have sudden impulses which you must learn to trust and follow, even when they seem unimportant and unreasonable. There will be people with whom you will have the prompting to get better acquainted, there will be letters to write, catalogues to send for, books to read.

Obedience to your subconscious must be unhesitating. You won't know until later, when you can trace the pattern by which you came to accomplishment, the reasons for these actions. But there will be a reason. Every prompting will carry you forward in the direction you are going, toward the goal which you have chosen.

The subconscious mind is doing the planning, but you are its instrument.

It has to work through you.

I'm not saying you are its only instrument; it will find others. There's a line of communication open between the subconscious of the girl who wants to go to college and the subconscious minds of those who can help that girl get there. The other person may not know he's helping, but your subconscious will know the use to which certain actions can be put and will prompt that person to the helpful action.

A business friend of your father's may be prompted to tell him how much his own daughter has improved as a result of further educational advantages. One of your instructors, noting your increased application to your studies, may be prompted to tell your mother that you are really college material.

Trust your subconscious; do as it directs. All sorts of things beyond your control will happen if you have done your part - planted the seed and kept it nourished.

Overcoming nervousness

I once knew a very young man whose first job was with an investment banking concern. It was quite a job for so young a fellow and it had him scared.

"This guy I've got to see tomorrow," he told me one day, "is up in millionaire row. I know I'll lose my nerve the moment I get into his outer office and the girl behind the desk puts her icy stare on me.

"I have an appointment. I know he's got some money he wants to get rid of. Just the same my voice will squeak when I give her my name and when she announces me, dripping disdain the way she does, I'll be licked before I get through his door."

I knew what he was going through; any businessman knows. Selling is a tough game. "What does he look like?" I asked, trying to think how best to build up his self-confidence.

"Oh, you know, the portly type," and the lad made a sketchy gesture with both hands around his middle that was very expressive.

"Lots of white hair. Eyebrows that stick out at you; black, too. And he growls."

I made a mental note of this young man's trick with word pictures. It could be valuable to him. I knew this man he was to interview, though I had never met him. The growling gave me the key.

"Yes, I see," I said. "He likes to scare the daylights out of timid people. That means he'd respect anybody who stood up to him. Suppose you saw him on the beach in a bathing suit; would you be afraid of him then?"

The boy laughed. "Bet he'd have hair on his chest," he said. And quite suddenly the tension had gone out of him. That was my cue. I knew exactly how to help him.

"Have you ever seen a dancing bear?" I pursued my idea.

"Sure," and his eyes gleamed: he was beginning to catch on. "They growl; but they're toothless so they can't bite."

"Imagine this prospect of yours with a *fez* on his head, hopping about first on one clumsy foot and then on the other," I went on painting his picture. "He's holding out a tambourine for people to drop in pennies or nickels."

I didn't need to say anything more; he'd licked his mental hazard already.

He told me afterwards that he walked past the girl at the desk, not seeing her, so intent was he in getting at that great bear inside. He gave her his name over his shoulder, his hand on the doorknob, which he turned in answer to her nod. And he sold the man $20,000 worth of securities. No argument.

Laughter had replaced fear. Ease, naturalness of manner in a really charming, alert, gifted young man did the rest. That was a lesson he never had to learn a second time.

The imagination he'd used on one prospect prompted him to destroy his fears of other difficult approaches by visualizations. He didn't need to call his subconscious to his aid. His conscious mind took care of him; or perhaps not. Probably it was his subconscious mind that dictated his picture-making.

He told me of another of his fancied transformation scenes. This time it was a gruff old man who wore white whiskers and had a vitriolic tongue.

"The old goat had me buffaloed," the young man said. "I knew he had money, but every time I met his scowl - and he was always scowling - I lost my nerve. Then my subconscious gave me my picture.

"I thought what a Santa Claus he would make; saw him all dressed up, sitting in a department-store window with a string of kids waiting their turn to sit on his knee. And of course I knew Santa Claus was a kindly old boy; nobody could be afraid of him. If he scowled, it would only be a joke.

"So I tackled him, and he was swell to me. I got a $50,000 order and he told me to come back next week and we'd go over his whole security list. That'll mean real business."

Executives are just plain people

This kind of experience is very common. Every executive of importance has elaborate office surroundings with secretaries and clerks; the show is very impressive. But if you are young, trying to find your feet in the business world, listen to your subconscious. It will tell you great executives are very human; or they wouldn't be in that position. They're just people. See them that way. They have the same virtues, the same faults as others.

And your subconscious is standing at your elbow to prompt you so that you will make the proper approach.

To one man it is all right to be brash and cocky; to another you'll please him only if you are polite. When you have learned to see in each man just another human being, the mental hazard will disappear. You'll understand him and he'll understand you. The more artificial barriers a man has put around himself, the easier he is to approach when you get to him.

A young lawyer once told me of an experience that illustrates this point. "I was pitted against a man of tremendous reputation," he said. "All younger men feared him and I admit I was frightened. But I'd learned the trick of handling myself, of giving my subconscious mind a call to take over. I shut my mind to everything about me. I shut my eyes and listened. 'You're just as good a lawyer as he is,' my subconscious mind assured me. 'He's been built up but take my word for it, you're the better man. You can lick him, and you will.'

"I listened; I repeated those phrases over and over. And when I opened my eyes I knew they were true. I knew I could lick him and I did.

"I've continued to use that ritual ever since. When I know I'm up against a tough case, or with an unfavorable jury, I hand over to my subconscious. It always works."

Of course it always works. You can depend on the directing power of your subconscious mind providing it can depend on you for obedience. That much cooperation you have to give.

A new way to sell cheese

A group of managers, assistant managers and butchers from a large chain store came to me once for a course of lectures. After a six weeks' period they decided to try out the principles I had been stressing. They would settle upon certain items and push the sale of those specified products mentally. After some debate they made out a program: one store would push cheese, another Hubbard squash, another salmon and a fourth rolled-roasts.

Each manager coached his clerks. As a customer approached his counter, the salesman was to make a mental picture, and hold it, of that person buying the article they were pushing. Of course the stores did not disregard the usual approaches; prominent displays were made. Yet the mental attitude of the clerk was the added sales factor.

Results were astounding. The store which was pushing cheese sold more in a day than they had in a six months' period previously. The shop which on Saturday specialized in rolled-roasts was sold out by noon. The one that had featured fresh salmon on Friday sold more than all the other stores in town combined. The one that had selected squash had to replenish its supply twice during the day. And each man who took those lectures was later in business for himself or in a much better job.

Your own mental approach to the matter in hand is vital; I can't repeat that too often.

Some people, it is true, use their mental powers without realizing what they are doing. But if we want uniform results, it is well to be self-conscious about the importance of giving over to our subconscious minds, of trusting and obeying.

A man who as a boy had learned the coffee roasting and blending business became convinced that he could do a better job at it than any other man so he went into business for himself.

He was a millionaire when he retired, still convinced that nobody else would ever equal his product. Belief like that, which must come from one's deep subconscious, reaches out like tendrils into the subconscious of others and convinces them.

Seeing what's before you

A printer whom I had given the job of getting out a small pamphlet for me came rushing, breathless, into my office. "I just had the queerest experience," he said. "I told myself that if this stuff worked the way you said it did in that pamphlet, I'd be able to find a parking space near your office when I came in this morning.

"I'd slowed down to let pedestrians pass and there wasn't a parking spot in sight. Then a car drew out from right in front of this office and I came in." He stopped, feeling sheepish, and added less excitedly, "Of course it was just one of those things."

"Why not try it again?" I suggested.

He did; and over a series of years he has continued to experience these so-called coincidences. Also, as a result of using this principle of visualization, this printer has more than trebled his business.

I've known others who had this same experience. A Unity student told me she never drives downtown without visualizing a parking space for herself near the place where she needs to stop; she has never failed to find it.

A woman dietician and instructor in a hospital told me: "The working of this power often frightens me. Every morning when I enter the business section on my way to the hospital, the traffic lights turn green and I go through without a stop. I'm getting to take it as a matter of course." Perhaps her subconscious takes over, synchronizing her driving pace with the timing of the lights.

The stockholders of an oil company that was experiencing great financial difficulties were told to make a mental picture of oil coming in from every spigot and hold it. They did and subsequently the company became a moneymaker.

Jimmy Gribbo, manager of prizefighters, made winners out of the boxers he handled by teaching them to visualize themselves as winners.

Do you really believe that all these occurrences are merely chance, coincidence? The game is still worth the trying. Dr. Matthews of the University of Chicago is credited with saying: "We influence events by very great desires, and there is psychological proof on ourselves of the effects of our own desires."

A too popular college girl suddenly realized that she was in danger of failing in a course on the Contemporary Novel. She hadn't done all the required reading and an important paper was overdue.

She was given an extension of time on the paper, but she couldn't write it until she had done that great mass of reading. Her father was a writer of some eminence. She adored him and didn't want to bring shame upon him, for she knew he would feel her failure deeply. So she refused all social engagements and went to work. But the time was short.

Then an out-of-town cousin wrote that she would be in town for a brief visit. The cousin was to be married soon; the girl was to be her bridesmaid. Naturally the visit would entail discussion and shopping expeditions. How could she refuse? Yet she couldn't spare so much as an afternoon or evening.

"I knew I was wrecked," she told me afterwards. "In desperation I went to work on my subconscious. I showed it a picture of my cousin delayed at home. I took her all over the house; I made her do all sorts of tasks I knew she was in the habit of doing. I didn't quite go so far as to put her mother to bed with a cold, but I considered it.

"Anyway, I got a telegram saying she'd have to put off her trip for another week. That saved me."

"Did you get a decent grade?" I asked.

"Of course," she said. "With a break like that, how could I not? My paper was 'brilliant.' I knew everything was going to be swell as soon as I got that visit postponed. But I've learned a lesson. I'll never let things get that close again. Dates aren't that important."

You may not think this girl's mental approach had anything to do with postponing her cousin's visit. I still repeat - it's worth trying.

My, you're looking well!

Here's one to try on your friends. Does some girl's sloppy carriage and glum facial expression annoy you? Start building her up *mentally.* Tell yourself what a good-looking girl she would be if she carried herself well. Tell yourself how charming she looks when she smiles. *Do this in your thoughts: don't say a word.* Do it every time you're with her.

And don't be surprised one day to see her coming toward you, a smile on her face and a lovely poise to her body. Belief in yourself or in someone else is very powerful.

Do you need this treatment yourself? Examine yourself in a full-length mirror. See yourself as you are. Then see yourself as you would like to be. Keep that picture of yourself before your eyes. The time will come when the two pictures will blend.

Chapter 9: FEAR AND IMAGINATION

FEAR, IN A CHILD OR IN A GROWNUP, IS BASICALLY AN IMAGINATION factor, and must be dealt with. Let's examine fear for a moment.

We all hate to go to the dentist. It isn't so much the actual pain as it is what we *think* we're going to feel. A Pittsburgh dentist, specializing in work for children, faced that problem. He fixed up a playroom with toys, blocks and sandboxes; he wanted the children to enjoy their visits to him.

When the young one was finally in the chair he let him play with turning on and off the electric drill. No child was afraid when he put the drill in his mouth since he could turn it off himself, at will.

This dentist's practice was enormous; he'd licked a mental hazard.

A barber met the same problem in the same way. He provided the child with books and mechanical toys and the child forgot that his hair was being approached by a man with instruments in his hand. The child was engrossed with what he held in his own hands and was no longer afraid.

Mental pictures can produce queer results. You get a telegram and before you open it you see all sorts of possible happenings. You see your sister - who has mentioned a slight indisposition in a recent letter - prostrate, dying. Or your father who is on an automobile trip is seen in all the gruesome details of a hospital's accident ward.

Then you open the telegram and find that a school friend is accepting your invitation to visit you during the holidays.

That habit of building up imaginary pictures of disaster is one that must be dealt with, for it is one way of bringing upon you or your friends and family the very troubles you are seeing for them in your mind.

We must learn the power of our thoughts both to avert and to precipitate events. Some people get a sinking feeling in the stomach every time the telephone rings. Yet all you have to do is to open the telegram, answer the telephone. Why nurse your fears?

Some imagination!

There's a story of a man who couldn't get a room in any hotel because a convention was crowding the town. Finally he was given a cot in a storage room. During the night he woke and felt stifled. He got up, groped for the window, couldn't open it, took his shoe and kicked out a pane of glass.

Then he went back to bed and slept soundly. In the morning he discovered that he had merely smashed the glass door into a closet. The window was still closed.

Margaretta West had a story in *This Week Magazine.* She told of returning on a troop ship from the South Pacific during the war. She was in a cabin with seventeen other women and because of blackout rules the portholes were closed. The cabin was stifling. But since the ship would not sail till morning, the women were given permission to open the portholes after everybody was in bed and the lights were out.

Miss West undertook the task of opening up, after which seventeen women breathed deeply in relief and went off to sleep. But in the morning they discovered that she had only opened the inner portholes; the outer ones had been tightly shut all night.

Science has proved in countless ways the effects of the workings of the imagination. A postage stamp, placed on the skin of a person who thinks it is a mustard plaster, will raise a blister. Animals, taught to associate food with the ringing of a bell, will secrete digestive juices at the sound of the bell, without the feeding. Sit at a lunch counter and see something that looks appetizing on a plate of your neighbor. Your mouth will water. Watch somebody peeling an onion, with tears streaming down his face. Your tears will start, too. Get food poisoning from, as you think, having eaten canned salmon. You'll get food poisoning again when you are fed salmon, even though this time it is fresh and perfectly safe. Try to whistle when a friend near you is sucking a lemon. Your mouth will pucker and you will be unable to make a sound.

Mark Twain, in his essay, *Concerning Tobacco,* said that men think they can tell a good cigar from a bad one, but they can't. He tells of borrowing from a wealthy friend a double handful of forty-cent cigars, which bore red and gold labels signifying their quality.

Mark Twain removed the labels and put the unbranded cigars into his own box. He was known as a smoker of the worst cigars. Then he passed these cigars to his friends after dinner. Everyone of them, after two or three puffs, threw aside the forty-cent cigars, so sure were they that they had been offered Mark Twain's own cheap brand.

Perhaps that isn't the whole truth: undoubtedly there is a difference in flavor between various grades of tobacco. And no doubt many among these men could have detected the difference. But their imaginations had convinced them they were being given Mark Twain's tobacco, and their imaginations won that battle.

Charles Fourier, a French philosopher of more than a century ago, declared that the future of the world would grow out of the brain of man: shaped, controlled and directed by the desires and passions by which men are moved. We are seeing his prophecy coming true.

"But that's silly" he said

You must constantly remind yourself as I am trying to remind you, of the tremendous power exerted by a *directed* imagination.

Because belief is the first essential in putting your subconscious to work for you, it is necessary to go back to that fundamental again and again.

The mechanical devices by which you feed suggestions into your subconscious in order to put that great force to work for the accomplishment of your desire vary with the individual. I have been urging you to cultivate the art of picture-making.

You want to be a person of arresting appearance and personality? See yourself that way. You want success in business? I have already called to your attention the devices by which executives stir themselves and their employees to achievement: portraits and statues of men who have achieved, slogans - anything that will serve as reminders to the subconscious mind which must, as we know, be reached through the conscious mind.

I've suggested card reminders, which you place where you see them daily, hourly. One man to whom I suggested this method laughed at me.

"It sounds so silly," he said. "Imagine me getting a new automobile by writing it down on a card."

"Try it," I advised him.

He did; and some months later showed me his new car.

One man to whom I had taught this method some years ago wanted, beyond any other accomplishment, a certain girl as his wife. He won her.

Another man's supreme ambition was wealth; in the course of time he accumulated a considerable fortune. To another came a beach cottage, and to another a new and larger home.

I've kept track of various students who have taken my courses and over a period of years not one of them has failed to attain to the desire upon which he had centered his thoughts and practiced the techniques I had advised.

Think - don't talk

I am going to repeat a caution I hinted at earlier. *Don't confide in this person and that the practices in which you are trusting to bring you your desired objective.*

Any writer will tell you that he loses interest in any project after he has talked it out with another person.

It has found adequate expression; why write it all down again? Why not go on to some new idea that is more interesting?

Secrecy gives power; concentration is more absolute if you keep your own council. I don't mean that you and your friends won't spend much time together, talking over your and their ambitions. I don't mean that you won't talk with your mother and father about that which is in your heart. You will want their advice and their help.

But don't talk about *these techniques* by which you are seeking to gain the cooperation of your subconscious mind in accomplishing your desire.

There is another reason for this caution to secrecy.

The subconscious mind of others might go to work against you. You might talk to someone who would think and say that the whole thing was ridiculous. Just that thought in the mind of another, if strongly expressed and believed, might weaken your own belief. Or you might have an ambition to which the person you've confided in was antagonistic, for a personal reason. Then he would put his subconscious to work fighting yours.

I cannot advise you too strongly to tell nobody about your use of cards, of visualization, of repetition to bring about your ambition. Consciously or unconsciously, the thought vibrations of others might go to work against you.

To illustrate: a doctor friend of mine during the war applied for a commission in the navy. Anticipating success, he closed his office and his friends gave him good-bye gifts and a party. But the commission did not come through for two years.

"That taught me a lesson," he said. "Never again will I tell anyone of my plans or desires."

I'm not saying that his commission would have come through more promptly if he had kept the matter between his conscious and his unconscious mind; but it seems to me very likely.

By talking he scattered his forcés; weakened his own power of concentration; weakened the force of his own subconscious in its attack upon the minds of those whose duty it was to see to the granting of commissions.

When you lose that close connection with the subconscious you are working to establish, you have to start all over again

Auto-suggestion helps

You will remember that I previously called your attention to chants, incantations, affirmations as a means of suggesting to your subconscious the desire of your conscious mind, as a means of stimulating the subconscious to activity. These repetitive words and phrases said silently or aloud are one method of convincing the subconscious mind that here is something needing attention.

Auto-suggestion, in no matter what form, is the only way to mold its pattern. The subconscious is extremely receptive and can be convinced of the propositions you present to it, be they true or false, positive or negative. And once the subconscious mind has accepted them, has them firmly embedded, it goes to work with all its faculties and energies to materialize them, to make them real in life.

Use simple statements

The simpler the words you use to impress your idea on your subconscious the better. Say you are unhappy and wish to change your state of mind. You won't need cards to remind you; simply say, "I am happy." Repeat it to yourself over and over. Use the same device if you want to impress on yourself such a need as, "I am a convincing speaker," or "I am friendly." By such simple affirmations you can change your whole mental point of view for the better.

But if the effects are to be permanent, the affirmations must be continued until the desired results are obtained and held.

The person with a fixed goal, a clear picture of his desire, an ideal held always before his conscious mind, causes it through repetition to be buried deeply in his subconscious mind and is thus enabled - thanks to its generative and sustaining power - to realize his goal in a minimum of time and with a minimum of physical effort.

Just pursue the thought unceasingly. Step by step you will achieve realization, for all your faculties and powers are being directed to that end.

Suppose you want a promotion. You are doing the work you have been given to do until it has become routine. You know you are ready for the next step.

Put your subconscious to work. Use the cards for frequent self-suggestion.

See yourself sitting at the desk the promotion would give you. Tell your subconscious you have the qualities as well as the desire for that next step up.

Your subconscious will bring it about. Either your boss will receive a mental reminder, will notice your work, consider your capabilities, or your subconscious will prompt you to go to him and speak to him about your desire. You will be nudged by your subconscious into such actions and words as will further your cause. If you keep it in your thoughts, conscious and subconscious, you will win.

It's like driving a nail in a board. The first tap puts the nail in place; but it takes a number of successive taps to drive the nail home. Never cease to believe that your subconscious is receiving and carrying out whatever you have instructed it to do.

Protect your subconscious

Two objects cannot fill the same space at the same time. Neither can two thoughts. You can't have a mind filled with negative thoughts or doubts if you have already filled it with positive, powerful, creative thoughts.

Picture your subconscious mind as a room with a single door to which only you have the key. It rests with you to decide what kind of thoughts shall enter through that door. So be very careful which kind you admit, negative or positive, for your subconscious mind will respond to the vibrations of the thoughts that are strongest in you.

Or compare your subconscious to a tank filled to the brim with clear, unadulterated water. You cannot put any object into that tank without displacing some of the water and causing it to overflow. If you permit negative thoughts, or fear or doubt to enter, they will displace the positive, creative thoughts. So long as you do not admit unfavorable vibrations, your subconscious mind will be safe from any perceptions of the senses. Keep your conscious mind filled with positive thoughts: thus you will be guarding that door, protecting your great powerhouse from any outside destructive forces.

Philosophers have always taught that we must keep busy if we want to be happy. When we are occupied at something which holds our interest, our minds are not open to roving and undesirable vibrations.

Occupy your leisure as well as your working hours with congenial occupations. Use your conscious mind to keep the subconscious mind from harmful influences.

But the subconscious mind is more than a treasure chest to be guarded. It is an active factor to be put to work. We get what we anticipate. Dale Carnegie used to tell of the great success of Howard Thurston, the magician. In going out on the stage Thurston would repeat over and over to himself: "I love my audience; I am going to give them the best that is in me." And he always did, with the result that his audience loved him. His success brought him in something like two million dollars.

Hammer it home

Repetition is the fundamental rhythm of all progress. There is a cadence to the universe. The chuff-chuff of the locomotive takes a train across the continent. The explosions that generate power in the automobile engine, the rocket gun, the robot bomb are repetitive. Constant, determined repetition breaks down resistance, sweeps away obstacles. Repeated auto-suggestion or hetero-suggestion makes you and others believe. It's what I am trying to do now: tap-tap on your conscious thought processes the ideas that will bring belief and power into your lives.

Professor Hugo Munsterberg, Harvard psychologist, said: "The value of repetition must be distinctly understood in the relation of the inner setting and the inner mental attitude."

In Paris, a famous institute teaches by playing the same phonograph record over and over: records asserting that you are in good health, that you have the power to overcome your difficulties.

Students in research laboratories have been taught the principle of repeating over and over to a sleeping child the suggestion to grow strong and well, to refrain from tantrums, to eat what it is given to eat, healing by suggestion whatever bad habits that particular child had formed. This is done in the belief that during sleep access to the subconscious mind is easier to effect.

Re-read your Roman history; you will find that Cato believed that Rome and Carthage could not both survive. In consequence of this conviction he ended every speech in the Senate with the words: "Carthage must be destroyed." He kept it up until Romans were saying it in their sleep. And of course we all know that Carthage, the greatest maritime power of the ancient world, was destroyed.

Many people allow themselves to be confused and frustrated by paying too much attention to the negative thoughts of others. They talk over their ideas with others and if they are told, "It can't be done," they accept the verdict. Close your mind to such negative thinking; counteract it constantly with your own positive thinking. Unless you do, you're defeated, sunk. But the place to combat those negative thoughts is in your mind. You must dominate your conscious and your subconscious mind before you can make your actions positive.

Don't follow the leader

Whether we know it or not, we are all victims of suggestion. We follow the path someone else suggests to us. We wear the kind of clothes we see others wear. We think the thoughts our newspapers and magazines tell us to think. In colleges where the honor system is practiced, numbers of students will cheat or not cheat in examinations in accordance with the leadership they are given.

Not only do we behave like sheep, we go around with our minds wide open and ready to reflect the thinking of those with whom we associate. The modern trend in architecture is no more than the reflection of a few original experimenters. Automobile styling follows the pattern of the accepted leader. Mass hypnosis is seen around us in every human activity.

Train yourself to observe. You will find that those people who make use of their subconscious powers - knowingly or not - have tremendous energy. They are people of strong convictions; they use their imaginations; they accomplish something in the world.

You will never find an inert, unenergetic, unimpressive personality in the man or woman, boy or girl who has learned to tap the depths of subconscious, dynamic living.

Have an active faith

"Faith without action is dead." That needs to be thought about. The basic principle of all our argument is the necessity for faith. But we need to realize the necessity to clothe our faith in action.

We live in a material world. We are spirit, mind, soul; but we are encased in and limited by physical bodies. The faith pattern of our thinking needs expression in the action pattern of our living. The fulfillment of our desires will bring us achievements perceptible by the senses. Our faith will show itself in our actions. Our secret and subconscious life inevitably will find an outlet in our behavior.

My aim is to train you to use your subconscious forces for the attainment of personal achievement. This means that your energies will be prompted by your subconscious to such actions as will bring you at length to your goal.

What you must learn to do is to follow out the ideas and make the contacts and take such measures as are dictated by your subconscious mind.

I always understood that Franklin D. Roosevelt constantly made use of his subconscious mind. He never looked "backward," but always "forward." Yesterday was a closed book to him. Kirke L. Simpson, an Associated Press staff writer, told of a party given for Mr. Roosevelt after he had been stricken with infantile paralysis. His friends, in recognition of Mr. Roosevelt's insistence that he would walk again, gave him a cane. They were going along with him in his belief that he would never need to depend on crutches.

And at that party Mr. Roosevelt sat all evening, Mr. Simpson said, with the cane cuddled against his shoulder. Now and again he would reach up and touch it. It was his reminder.

You see what he was doing? His fingers on the cane was his message to his conscious mind to send its command to his subconscious mind. He was telegraphing his intention to walk again.

A doctor wrote Mr. Roosevelt, seeking advice on the treatment for infantile paralysis. Mr. Roosevelt suggested gentle exercise, massage, and sunbathing. "But," he added, "more important than most therapy is a belief on the patient's part that he will eventually recover."

Here we see in the case of disease both the magic of believing and the power of suggestion. Suggestion by repetition, suggestion by mental pictures -suggestion by any method you can devise - this is an essential technique **in** training your subconscious to serve you.

And always and foremost comes faith, belief.

Chapter 10: SEEING IS BELIEVING

IF, BY THIS TIME, I HAVE FAILED TO CONVINCE YOU OF what it can mean to you and your future to master the art of using the powers of your subconscious mind, this chapter will be nothing but gibberish to you.

You cannot build up for yourself a technique to be used in releasing these latent forces to work for you unless you believe in them.

Granted, then, that you do believe; granted that you have formulated for yourself some definite ambition, that you realize the power there is in suggestion, that you realize the importance of repetition and of visualization as means toward that end; granted these points, we are ready for the suggested techniques that are to be given in this ensuing chapter.

Follow the rules

I realize that you are in the difficult position of any student who must follow more or less blindly a course of action dictated to him, in which he believes, but in which he has not yet had the experience to feel at ease. This is the route of progress.

If you are a student deeply interested in modern history, you have to accept the assurance of your instructor that it will pay you to take the time for a detailed examination of the happenings of early civilizations. If your student mind is turned in the direction of philology, you admit, perhaps reluctantly, the necessary preparation Latin and Greek must be familiar companions; all languages, in fact, are no more than your required tools.

I am asking you to follow my suggestions willingly, accepting, believing.

In that way proof will come, the proof which success brings.

Let us say that you have just graduated from college. For the first time in your life you are on your own. Your parents have done all they can for you; there are younger brothers and sisters coming along with the expense of their advanced training to be met. You must go to work.

So you're going to work

What kind of job do you want? You've majored, perhaps, in English Literature, or History, or Psychology, or Economics. You realize that you will never get very far in any of these lines without further study, without advanced degrees. It is obvious, then, that you must find work near to some institution of learning where you can continue your studies; work in which the hours are somewhat flexible, permitting you to carryon such continuance of your student days.

A teaching position in or near a university town would meet these conditions. But you must plan more accurately than that. What you need is not a position near a university, but near *the* university which would offer the best in the advanced work you want to follow, which would carry you nearest to the goal you have set for yourself: the long-distance goal, I mean, of supremacy in your chosen field. Your goal of finding the right position at this point in your forward march is only one step along that path.

Believe. Belief that you will find that perfect position which you need at this stage in your career must be absolute. *Know* it with every atom of your being. Never admit doubt to enter your conscious thinking.

Then use your reminder cards

This brings you to Rule Number 2. Get your cards to work. Cut your prompt-card phrase down to the simplest language. *University town* might be all you would need.

Or, if you already know what particular university would best fit your wishes, put the name of that specific university on your cards. Just the sketch of a main building would do; or initials; anything that would bring to your mind at a glance the whole picture of your desired object.

Again I must repeat the caution: don't talk!

By this I do not mean, as I have explained previously, that you should refrain from discussion (with your parents, with your instructors, with friends who might give you necessary information) at the aim you have set up for yourself. Naturally they will know that you want a teaching position. Indeed, you will need letters of recommendation and other "assists." But *do not talk of this technique* whereby you are employing all the powers of your own subconscious mind to bring about your desire.

The thinking of your conscious mind can be helped by asking advice and information as to which school would best answer your needs; you wouldn't know that without such consultations. But when your conscious mind has made its decision, then you must stop talking and THINK.

The problem of how to obtain the desired appointment is now being given over by you to your subconscious mind. What it will prompt you to do as a means toward that end must be obeyed; and if you were talking, planning, listening to others you might not realize those promptings.

If you did not hear them, if your mind was too busy to receive them, you would let go by some necessary step in your progress. Your subconscious mind would be thwarted, might even cease to act for you.

You must keep the channel open: your conscious mind must be ready to receive and obey its promptings. Therefore, I repeat, after you have decided upon your aim, stop talking with others about that aim. Give all your conscious energy to feeding into your subconscious mind the promptings which will induce it to take over and act for you.

You must believe. You must use your cards continuously. Keep them where they will prompt you, daily, hourly. Again and again and again you must repeat, consciously, your instructions to your subconscious mind: the name of the university town in which you wish to obtain a teaching position.

There are always certain steps which must be taken and which you would know without any subconscious prompting. You must make application for the position you desire; you must fulfill all requirements dictated in the answer to that application.

But after that is done, you must cooperate with your own subconscious in the obtaining of the appointment. Never forget how important it is to put all your powers into *thinking,* not into *talking.*

Through the looking glass

Here is another device that may help you. I call it *the mirror technique.* Before I explain it I want to tell you how I happened to discover it.

I was once the dinner guest of a very wealthy man who owned many patents covering logging and sawmill machinery. I was only one of a number of newspaper publishers, bankers and industrial leaders whom he had invited to his suite in a hotel in order to explain to them a new method he had devised for mill operations.

Wanting the cooperation of his guests, he had provided lavishly in the way of liquor. It wasn't long before our host himself was intoxicated. Just before dinner was served I noticed him reeling into the bedroom of the suite and, thinking he might need assistance, I stepped to the door between the two rooms; hence I was a witness of the queer incident which followed.

I saw this man literally pull himself together, sober himself up. It was a remarkable exhibition. He was standing before the mirror on his dresser, holding himself erect by grabbing the edge of the bureau with both hands. And he was mumbling to himself in the way a drunken man often does.

At first I didn't realize what he was saying, but gradually his enunciation cleared up and the words became more and more distinct.

"John," he said, talking to his image in the glass, "you old fool! They tried to get you drunk, but you're not. You're sober; cold sober. This is your party and you've something to say that is important. You've got to be sober."

He repeated these words over and over, staring himself straight in the eyes. And I watched the transformation come over him. His body became erect; he no longer had to support himself by gripping the edge of the bureau. The muscles in his face tightened. The bleared look left his eyes.

The whole performance took, perhaps, five minutes. In my experience as a newspaperman, and more particularly as a police reporter, I had had many opportunities to observe the behavior of drunken men. This was the first time I had witnessed such a sight: a man, so tipsy he could hardly walk without staggering, becoming cold sober within the space of five minutes.

When we were all seated in the dining room with our host at the head of the table, I could see no sign of his former state other than a slight flush. His behavior, his conversation was that of a man who had drunk no more, say, than a couple of cocktails. After the dinner he was able to present his new plans clearly and convincingly.

It was not until some time after this incident that I understood its significance. I had not then been studying the uses to which the subconscious mind could be put and the methods by which its cooperation could be induced.

But when I had begun my studies into this subject, the picture came back to me of a man consciously dictating to his subconscious mind, staring himself in the eyes meantime, what he wanted that subconscious mind of his to do for him. I had seen him talk himself out of drunkenness into sobriety.

That taught me the usefulness of this particular technique and I have used it, myself, many times since, though not, I must explain, for that particular object. I have used it on other people with very unusual results.

Facing trouble

For years, now, people have been coming to me with their troubles and a surprising number of them have been women. Now women, practically all of them, are likely to start their stories with weeping spells. And of course I have to deal with those tears before I can get on with the interview. So I experimented with this man's mirror idea. I would hand a woman a looking glass; or, better still, I would stand her up in front of a full-length mirror and I would bid her look at herself.

I would ask her to look into her own eyes and ask her what she saw there, a crybaby or a fighter. This always brought results. No woman gives way to a spell of weeping before someone else if she is made to realize what she looks like: pride and shame always ended that phase of the interview. (Of course, in this case the suggestion needed to go no further than the conscious mind.)

Great orators, preachers, actors and statesmen have used this mirror technique for years. Winston Churchill, according to Drew Pearson, never made a speech of importance unless he had made it first to himself before the mirror. And while he may not have realized that he was enlisting the cooperation of his subconscious mind by so doing, nevertheless that was the result. Woodrow Wilson, Pearson declared, did the same thing. In reality this is a supercharging method of stepping up the subconscious forces so that when the speaker appears before his audience, those forces flow out and affect his listeners.

Seeing yourself

By using a mirror in rehearsing a speech you are going to deliver, you are creating a picture of yourself; you are hearing your own words and the sound of your own voice; probably you are also visualizing the audience to whom you will be talking.

By looking in the mirror you increase the mental vibrations with the result that the force and meaning of your words will penetrate quickly to the subconscious minds of your audience.

I knew Billy Sunday, the evangelist, in his heyday and I was puzzled by his power and personal magnetism. He was able to influence people to a remarkable degree.

At that time I knew nothing of this science of mind power. But Eric Sevareid, Columbia Broadcasting System commentator, gave me the answer to this puzzle in his book, *Not So Wild a Dream.* He tells how, as a young newspaper reporter, he had secured an interview with Billy Sunday.

He bounded about the hotel room, now peering intently out of the window, with one foot on the sill, now grasping the dressing table firmly in both hands while lecturing to his reflection in the mirror.

Whether Billy Sunday knew the principles back of this mirror technique or not I couldn't say, probably he did not. But he knew how to use it. And what such men as Winston Churchill and Woodrow Wilson and Billy Sunday did instinctively, you can train yourself to do consciously.

Sell yourself your ideas

Every sales manager of any big concern, trying to instill into his salesmen the art of salesmanship, has used the expression: "If you can convince yourself, you can convince the other fellow."

Every great mass movement in history, whether religious or military, has been started off, sparked by someone aflame with belief in his cause. Converts by the thousands are drawn after such a leader. You need not be a student of psychology to realize that enthusiasm is contagious and can be readily transmitted if one is bursting with it.

The mirror technique is a simple and effective method by which you can sell yourself, can strengthen your own belief, can intensify the power of your enthusiasm, can convince yourself of your own worth and ability.

When you stop to consider this mirror technique in the light of our studies of mental accomplishments, you will realize what a master method we have at hand for releasing the mighty forces of the subconscious mind and employing it to influence those with whom we have to deal.

For we are all engaged in the science of salesmanship whether we know it or not. If we are not selling things, objects, wares, we are selling our ideas, our personalities.

Sell your family

All human relationships are based on selling in one form or another. We engage in it every time we attempt to persuade someone to our way of thinking.

You are "selling" your mother the idea that you need a new dress. You are "selling" your father the idea that you need - must have the use of the family car for a particular evening. Unless you can win your mother or your father to your way of thinking, you've lost out. Your attack has been an effort to bring one or the other of them to your way of thinking, and your failure indicates your need of new arts in the science of salesmanship.

I have often been called upon to work with business and sales organizations on the problem of increasing business. In a pie-making organization I had mirrors fastened to the inside of the back doors of all trucks. That meant that the first thing the driver-salesman would see on opening that door to get out the goods for delivery would be that mirror.

It would stop him; there is something very arresting about suddenly seeing yourself in a mirror. Then I instructed him to pause, look himself in the eye, and tell himself how many pies he was going to sell the customer on whom he was about to call. Put it high, I told him, and see a picture of that number of pies lying on his counter when you leave his store.

One driver told me that for months he had been trying to sell one woman restaurant-owner without success. That first day of the mirror- on-the-door experiment he sold her ten pies. And from that time on he sold her an average of fifteen.

In another manufacturing concern I had mirrors placed in the room where the employees left their hats and coats. Over the mirrors I pasted slogans, a different one every day - I wanted to compel each of them to stare at himself in the mirror for so long as it took him to read that day's prompting: "We're going to win," or "We've got guts: let's prove it." Sometimes I would use soap to write the slogan on the face of the mirror.

Results were so startling that subsequently we added mirrors to the doorframes of the main office so that the last thing a man saw as he left was himself in that mirror. It straightened shoulders, lifted chins, put smiles on glum faces.

I also placed mirrors on the frames of all the calendars of all the desks in the executive offices. I wasn't relying on the salesmen in that concern to do all the right thinking. They trebled and quadrupled their business. And salesmen whose income had never exceeded $300 a month were soon earning $1,000 monthly. Incredible? No, it isn't, because it's true.

How to use the mirror technique

Now let's outline this technique as it applies to you and your ambition.

Stand in front of your mirror. It need not be a full-length mirror but it should be large enough to show you a portion of your body as well as just your head. You know what the army means when it calls you to attention; stand that way. Erect, heels together, stomach in, chest out and head up.

Now breathe deeply three or four times until you feel in yourself a sense of power, of strength and determination. It is amazing what an upright posture can do for anyone of us.

Next: look into the depths of your own eyes. Tell yourself what it is that you want. Name it aloud - whatever it is that you have decided to go after. See your lips move. Listen so that you hear the words. Repeat it over and over. And make a regular practice of this ritual; go through this routine at least twice each day, particularly mornings and evenings.

You will be surprised at the results. If you think you might augment those results by pinning up slogans that particularly appeal to you, do that. But take them down afterwards. I cannot repeat too often the caution that all of this routine by which you enlist your subconscious into serving you and your desire must be strictly between you and your own conscious mind.

You probably think I am being super-cautious. But I assure you that any careless talk whereby you enlist the subconscious minds of others against you could defeat your purpose. The one to whom you talk might be actively antagonistic: or at least might laugh at you and so weaken your own faith in the process in which you are engaged. Keeping quiet, keeping the channel between your conscious and your subconscious mind open is essential.

Don't waste your forces. Don't give the subconscious minds of others a chance to get at you. Be very serious and faithful in following through. If you use slogans, point them definitely at what you have previously visualized, what you want to bring to reality.

Even when you are away from your mirror, you will be able to see the picture of yourself gazing into your own eyes, demanding the assistance from your subconscious that it can give. This practice will develop self-confidence in you in a matter of days. You will build up a force within yourself that you have never realized you had.

Stare your worries away

Consider again the case of the young college graduate who needs a position within striking distance of some university in which he can do graduate work.

He (or she) has received from a teacher's agency a notification of such a place. He has fulfilled all the preliminary requirements. Now an interview with the superintendent of schools in that particular locality has been arranged. So far his conscious mind could take him without recourse to his subconscious.

But he is worried. There will be other applicants for the position. That he knows, for it is a desirable appointment. They may be as qualified, or more so than he. Too much hangs on the impression he will make in the coming interview. It will be his one opportunity to sell himself.

And so I would strongly advise him to resort to the mirror technique. He should let his subconscious mind help him, let it approach the subconscious mind of the man who is to interview him.

Remember? Stand in front of your mirror; breathe deeply; wait for confidence to flow through you. Then tell your subconscious mind what you want. Never mind about preparing the arguments in your favor - they are all in those preliminary papers that have been submitted; if they weren't satisfactory you wouldn't have been called for the interview.

What is wanted now is an impression of your personality. Your scholarship is satisfactory but what about the carrying power of your real self; will prospective students like you, listen to you, be open to receive what you are there to give?

Don't plan what you will say - such rehearsal gets between you and the promptings of your subconscious mind. The point to be impressed on this superintendent is what you *are.* See yourself as victorious, triumphant. Believe you will get this job, which you want and need. *Believe* it. Let your subconscious mind know that you believe it, that you are trusting it to deliver. Look yourself in the eyes in your mirror and *know.*

Does this sound silly? Every idea presented to the subconscious mind is going to be reproduced in its exact counterpart in objective life.

The picture your subconscious mind sees as you stand before your mirror is the picture that school superintendent will see when you enter his office. Give your subconscious mind a picture and it will supply the power to make that picture real.

The eyes have it

We all talk about the eyes of our friends. We look into their eyes to discover their moods, for the mouth may smile while the eyes remain somber. Notice your own eyes. As you practice before your mirror you will see them change. Their expression will become more alive; you will see in them an increase in power.

By their growing intensity you will be able to realize how you are succeeding in impressing upon your subconscious the picture, the idea that you are striving to register. And this added power and intensity will carry over into your daily life. Your friends will begin to recognize in you an increase of force and personality.

Emerson has told us that every man carries in his eyes the exact indication of his rank. If you wish to stand high, to be among the foremost of your associates, to be able to influence those about you, practice the mirror technique.

As your self-confidence develops, so will the expression of your eyes deepen and bear witness to others that you are someone to be reckoned with.

Your mirror will do other things for you. Besides intensifying your look of power and personality, it will bring about an increase in physical attractiveness.

If you have poor posture, are slovenly in your walk and appearance, your mirror will tell you so. A dominating personality, someone who is going places and is able to succeed in whatever undertaking he has chosen doesn't look like that. You must build up more than the expression in your eyes. Your whole body must respond to that ambition you are asking your subconscious to fulfill.

Indeed this increase in physical appeal is one of the weapons your subconscious is prompting you to contribute to its ultimate success.

Your mirror shows you what you look like to the people around you: to your family, to your friends, to the strangers you happen to meet. But it is within your power so to use your mirror as to make that person, whom they see, over into the person you would like them to see.

If you intend to become a person of power you must add to your picture the look of a person of power. Whatever you have chosen for your role in the drama of life you must act before your mirror. I am not speaking to your vanity. I am talking to that deep, inner self which is your true self and which only needs your cooperation to take over and be visible to all with whom you come in contact.

We hear a great deal of loose, uninformed talk about "intuition," or "hunches." Some psychologists will tell you that these ideas that come to you "out of the blue" are in reality subconscious promptings from the accumulated knowledge not only of our own experiences but of those of other people; are something we can tap out of the great, nebulous mass of the universe itself. It is all very vague and impractical.

Certainly many scientists have ideas of procedure come to them in flashes of intuition. Writers, artists, composers all confess to a dependence on inspiration, illumination from the subconscious mind.

They are often aware of truths and yet have no knowledge of having previously planted those seeds in the mind. Obviously this is a subject about which we are going to know a great deal more as time and experimentation continue.

I don't claim to have solved the theory of the subconscious. I know it is there; so do you. I have worked out a pattern, a set of techniques whereby its power becomes available for use, if you choose to follow along with me. I ask you to accept my suggestions, to practice them, to prove to yourself their workability.

Take them; use them; let them help you to find the answers to your personal problems.

Chapter 11: YOUR MONEY PROBLEMS

ONE OF THE TOUGHEST PROBLEMS CONFRONTING MOST people is the problem of money.

Young people need money to pay for their education, to start out in business, to get married. Fathers of families need money more and more all the time to meet the growing demands of their families and of their businesses.

All right, we'll concentrate our discussion briefly on the meeting of this money lack. And I won't give you, by way of an answer, the picture of walking the street and picking up packages of thousand dollar bills, though I've heard of such happenings. I have never had much faith in the easy way out of any difficulty. I've had to earn what I've won from life.

No, don't concentrate on the picture of a roll of bills lying at your feet on the sidewalk. You'd have to turn them over to the police anyway, if you're honest.

Concentrate on feeding to your conscious mind, and so to your subconscious mind, the idea of your need. Think it over first; analyze your need. Don't hurry your thinking; be very sure that the picture you settle upon is a true picture.

If you had a thousand dollars you could buy yourself a part in a going concern in which you believe, with which you would like to be affiliated. Concentrate on one thousand dollars. Write $1,000 on your cards; place them where you will see them frequently. Repeat to yourself your need of that exact sum. Say it aloud at every opportunity. Tell yourself about it while you stare into your own eyes in the mirror. Your subconscious mind will go to work on the problem of supplying your need.

It will prompt you to such action as will lead, eventually, to your possession of that exact sum of money. And all the time that you are engaging in these techniques, believe; plan and act as though the matter were already accomplished.

Or is it the money for your first year in college you are working for? Use your cards; use your mirror; use your opportunities for repetition. And plan and act as if the money were already in the bank. Examine catalogues; select your courses. The money will come.

It will be the same technique, no matter what your desire. Get the picture of what you want clear; no blurred edges. Keep telling yourself that you are going to get it. Go to work on yourself; keep the idea ever before your conscious mind; keep feeding it to your subconscious mind. And don't get the idea that your only part in bringing about your desire is one of watchful waiting.

Do your part

You are the subconscious mind's chief agent. If you are asking for money, start saving. Keep open to the suggestions of your subconscious mind about ways and means of acquiring money.

When you are a businessman, at work on the problem of finding additional capital for expansion, in addition to the techniques needed to get the subconscious mind to work on the problem, start planning your expansion. Know what you mean to do with that money when you get it. Use all the intelligence your conscious thinking has.

This subconscious mind of yours isn't just an Aladdin lamp sprite.

You need to do more, much more, than express a desire. Your subconscious mind will tell you what to do; but you must be alert to hear and quick to obey.

A young woman with no previous training in the way of making a living was suddenly left alone. Her only asset was a fairly large-sized house. She knew about this system of calling upon all her own mental faculties to solve her difficulties. She applied them.

She knew how to cook and keep house; her mother had trained her. The obvious idea that came to her almost at once was to turn her house into a money making plant by taking roomers and boarders.

Many have tried that, as we all know, and failed. It is easy for an inexperienced young woman to fill her house with nonpaying guests. It is easy for her to hire more help than the amount of business warrants. It is easy to set an extravagant table. Spending money is always easy. But this young woman measured her own inexperience against the wisdom of her subconscious mind.

She built up in herself the power of an immediate reaction to applicants for her hospitality. She "knew" whom to take, whom to reject. Her conscious mind, in close communion with her subconscious, reminded her that with no capital to back her she must keep her establishment solvent. She did all her own buying and she learned the advantages of early morning, wholesale selections. She must be her own cook, the most expensive help item in such a business. For the rougher cleaning she could afford to hire someone but she was never above any menial task.

Easy? By no means. It was a grueling schedule she was following. But she began to make money, and she did not change her frugal manner of work and expenditure. Instead she invested her savings.

Two years later she sold her house with its established business at a profit. And she bought a larger house. She selected a location directly across from a well-known men's club, feeling sure her reputation for fine cooking would bring her much of the club's overflow business. It did. Again she prospered, and now she felt justified in hiring adequate help.

You say any intelligent woman could have done the same? I am sure of it; only what do you mean by "intelligent"? Just what *I* mean, I am sure: a young woman with a self-directed and disciplined mind. In other words, a young woman able to employ her own subconscious mind as a guide.

But the interesting fact about this woman's career to me was that she never made any of the usual mistakes. Her employees did not cheat her; her guests did not walk out owing her money. Her investments did not fall apart suddenly. And this unvarying success seems to me proof that a person who permits the subconscious mind to cooperate with the conscious mind, who follows its precepts, attains his objective.

He "sold" himself to the landlord

Here's another case of success attained in a period of less than ten years by the intelligent application of these principles of guided intelligence.

A corner druggist had gone into bankruptcy. The fixtures were owned by the owner of the building, most of the stock by the wholesale house. A young pharmacist heard about the location but had no funds with which to proceed. What did he do? He "sold" himself to both landlord and wholesaler.

How? You know how. If you have convinced your subconscious mind of the rightness of the picture you are holding of yourself, it will guide you in convincing others. He "saw" himself as the new owner of that particular drugstore. And he was able to make those men see it his way.

He reopened the store; his wife helped him. She served behind the soda counter; she was cashier and pinch-hitter wherever needed. Together they did all the work of the store. And they began to prosper.

For a long time this young man had been interested in a preparation which he thought would help people, but he didn't have the funds to put it on the market. One day he decided to talk with the owner of his building, a man of considerable wealth. So thoroughly did he believe in his plan that he had no trouble in convincing the owner who agreed to organize a company and advance $5,000 of his own money immediately.

For months this druggist bottled the preparation himself, working nights after the store was closed in the basement of an empty house. People bought it in increasing quantities and the business expanded.

In a few years this young man had paid off his landlord and his own profits had exceeded $50,000. Soon his income reached the $100,000 a year bracket. He and his company now own the building in which he started in the basement.

Here's the story of another business success. This man, as he told me, had been hanging on by his teeth. Then one night, as he was going home from church "the light hit me. Something led me to search for an old formula my father had used in preparing a lotion or tonic to be used in all barber shops and beauty parlors."

He found the formula; began gathering bottles from junk shops and scrap piles. He washed the bottles and they became his first containers. Then he went personally from barbershop to barbershop, from beauty parlor to beauty parlor.

So sure was he of the value of his product that he gave up his small paying job and opened up a plant of his own. His product became widely known. Soon he had his own sales organization and wholesalers, too, were pushing the lotion. Another illustration, you see, of the magic of believing, of trusting that "something" which tells you what to do.

THE MAGIC OF BELIEVING FOR YOUNG PEOPLE

First, an idea

Get-rich stories are, to most of us, as exciting as were the fairy tales of our childhood. But we must remember that everything on a material plane was first an idea in somebody's mind. All businesses, all fortunes are the outgrowth of an idea, the working of someone's imagination followed by action. And the success of that action comes, whether one knows it or not, from the coordination of the subconscious with the conscious mind.

For years I have watched the progress of the Jantzen Knitting Mills, makers of the famous Jantzen swimming suits. I have seen this concern grow from practically nothing but an idea to an organization that circles the globe. And the success story behind it rivals any told by Horatio Alger.

J. A. Zehnbauer, president of the company and chairman of the board, has given me permission to quote from a letter he wrote me:

As you say, some people seem to possess an indefinable something which spurs them on to a successful and a happy life; while others apparently work hard but without that something in their characters which brings them satisfaction and success.

I have never tried systematically to develop this indefinable spirit but I believe it has been developed in me by my parents, and especially by my mother, who promptly fought our inclination as youngsters to say, "I can't do this," or "I can't do that," by saying to us that of course we can do anything that anybody else can do, and all that was necessary was to tackle the job and keep on trying until we had mastered it; that we would then be ready to tackle a bigger job; that we must shrink from no job because it was great or small.

Then she was constantly resisting our inclination as youngsters to complain or growl about something. "Don't grumble," she would say, "but think what a privilege it is to live in such a wonderful world. Instead of complaining brace up and keep smiling and enjoy the blessings at hand."

There were four youngsters in our family, three boys and one girl. We have always been exceptionally happy and I attribute it to the training of our parents; mother with her constant admonitions and father corroborating her by saying often, "Always look on the bright side, never on the dark side of things."

I am afraid we must admit that such training in these days is rare, perhaps nonexistent. Mr. Zehnbauer realizes that, for his letter continues:

If one has not been fortunate enough to have the advantages of such influences, I can see where it would take a great amount of self-discipline and training to bring one up to the point of view which you clearly point out is necessary to get the most out of life. Regardless of one's present circumstances, I am sure the application of your science would be valuable to him.

Don't fool yourself

There are no short cuts. In our world today competition is unusually keen and naturally the person best prepared for a certain position is the one most likely to get it. This sounds obvious, of course; I'm saying it to remind you that mind power will not avail against such odds.

If you are honest in seeking the cooperation of your subconscious mind, one of the promptings you would receive would be the need to prepare yourself for that at which you are aiming; it would bid you seek the necessary training as the first step toward your ambition.

A young man cannot step out of the army into a position of leadership in, say, an industrial plant without coming up the ladder. But mind power can direct that climb, can speed his rise, can win from him his best by way of concentration and ability.

You must be sure of your own ability to fill the spot to which you aspire. How can you be "sold" on yourself unless you have confidence in your own equipment and capabilities? Your first step toward the job you want must be to fit yourself to fill it worthily.

Don't try to substitute mind power for training and ability. An executive said to me once, "The difficulty with most people seeking employment is that they are so wrapped up in themselves that they make no effort to impress a prospective employer with what they can do to help him. They overlook the fact that the man across the desk is only interested in finding out how useful the applicant can be to him."

Now that is a situation from which mind power would save you. If you are the boy or girl across the desk from this executive and if you want the job very much indeed, tell your conscious mind to notify your subconscious mind that this is important to you, ask that you be prompted to make the right approach.

You would have been thinking as you entered this man's office, "I am the person you want. I can serve you. I am competent. I will be an asset to you. You will see it in my eyes; you will see it in my body as I walk across the floor and sit down in that chair you are indicating for me to take. You are going to want me for this job for you are going to realize that I can be of use to you."

Your thoughts are showing

If you are thinking that way you will walk that way, sit that way, talk that way. You'll get the job and - if you are competent - you will hold it. But of course that is a mistaken "if" clause.

You are trusting yourself to the leading your subconscious mind gives you and you wouldn't be applying for this job if you were not fitted to perform its duties satisfactorily to your employer and to yourself. Guidance will always come from your subconscious if you keep the channel open and are in communion with it at all times.

This is very important; you owe it to yourself to keep that closeness alive, to keep your subconscious mind and your conscious mind in agreement.

For that old saying is really true: "If you do not follow your own thoughts, then you will follow the thoughts of the fellow who follows his."

Don't disregard this warning. Life is being lived by everyone on a mental plane even more than on a physical one. If you are not the ruler of your own spirit, the spirit of someone else will rule you. You cannot close off access to your subconscious mind from the outside unless you are controlling its activities from the inside.

You will be master of your own soul or someone else will master you. You will be in this life a leader or a follower and you can't prevent yourself from being a follower unless you take over the responsibility of being the leader, at least of your own thinking.

I am being as emphatic as I know how to be, for this is a truth which we so often neglect. Our own lazy-mindedness makes us unwilling to accept the responsibility.

You must use your own creative abilities or they will be used by someone else, perhaps to your undoing.

Do your own thinking: that is the only way in which you will attain to adequate living.

We really have to face this problem of coming to terms with our own subconscious minds. It isn't a matter of choice. You use your powers, or you are used by others.

Cultivate your communication; instruct your conscious mind to keep the door open to the promptings of the subconscious, to the so-called "hunches" or "intuitive flashes." Happiness, success, a rich and fulfilled existence will come to you by no other method of procedure.

The answer might come at any time

Great leaders, industrialists, inventors, artists all openly declare their faith in the ideas that come to them in their odd moments of relaxation.

When you have turned your problem over to your subconscious mind and very much want instruction, ask it - just as you are falling asleep at night - to give you the answer in the morning. It may even wake you during the night to instruct you in the course of action you must follow. Or you may find that you will have to wait and the answer will come while you are preoccupied with something else.

The subconscious mind is very independent in its procedures. But be quick to grasp the suggestion when it comes; waste no time in following through.

Let us say that you have applied for a certain position which you want very much. And your subconscious comes through with the suggestion that you call up a man who, so far as you know, has no connection with the person from whom you want to get the decision.

Call him up. You've nothing to lose, even if the idea seems crazy. And you won't know, though your subconscious may, that a word from him will influence the other man's yes or no. Obey your hunch and do it at once.

A "hunch" is something different

Here I must put in another word of caution. This system is not a gambler's bonanza. A lot of people bet on cards and dog races and horse races, or on the stock market. And a lot of people have what they call "hunches." A man fifty-six years old and this is 1956. So there's his "lucky" number: fifty-six. He looks at a roadside sign in which the word "Vixen" is used: and there's a horse running in the third race with the name "Vixen." He'll put his money on that horse: but, win or lose, that's not the way the subconscious works. We're talking about something fundamentally different.

Faith in that sort of "hunch" can lead into all kinds of trouble. We are talking about an ambition well considered and carefully weighed, planted by the conscious mind in the subconscious mind; planted, nurtured, watered, fed. When the subconscious mind has worked out the problem it begins to communicate with you by means of sudden thought flashes. That is a scientific approach. It is not the way to get the name of a horse on which to bet.

I don't want to labor this point but I do want you to realize that this is not a system for attaining to riches and fame overnight.

This is, I hope, a key that will fit the lock to a door opening on a long, bright passage with accomplishment and success at the end of the journey. You have, by your conscious thinking, put - away off there at your rainbow's end - a certain wonderful dream. You have entrusted that dream to the keeping of your subconscious mind. You are trusting, believing, that your own subconscious will bring about the embodiment of that dream in reality. It will. If you have faith, if you persist, you will reach your goal.

How long the route or how difficult, how much patience and hard work may be required, no man can foretell. Those are details that will vary with the facts.

If you are a boy who has decided to become a surgeon you have years of preparation ahead of you. What your subconscious can do for you is to save you from the mistakes we all make when we rely on our own half-baked impulses. It will save you time, and perhaps heartache.

If you are a girl with an ambition to be an actress, you have a difficult way ahead of you. Success in the arts comes only as the result of sacrifice, devotion, hard work and talent.

Many people will add "luck" to that.

But you see I don't believe in "luck."

I believe in the rule of the subconscious. If you are being led by your subconscious you will find that all your efforts are made to count. You will obtain the right sort of dramatic training, suited to your particular gifts. You will be directed to the right stock companies or summer theaters for your preliminary experience and training. You will make contacts that will be helpful to you.

"Hunches" - in the wrong sense of the word - will never take you where you want to go. But "guidance" from your subconscious will.

You furnish the ambition

This science will prove useful only to such young people as already know what they want of life. Your subconscious will not furnish your ambitions; those come from your character. They are framed into words and pictures by your conscious thinking. Use all the abilities of your conscious mind before settling upon a goal.

Observe the lives of others; talk with people who seem to have attained something in life; analyze those who are obviously unhappy failures. Examine your own gifts and capabilities. You aren't the man for a scientific laboratory if you are unable to move with ease in the intricacies of mathematical formulas. The life may look glamorous, but it is not for you.

You'll not succeed as a dress designer if you have never been able to choose your own clothes so as to give an effect of taste and distinction.

Be reasonable: place before yourself a goal that is not only attractive, but that is within the capabilities you feel within yourself.

Know what you want; settle upon it with all the keenness and wit you possess. Then be willing to pay the price to get there. And the price will be patience, hard work, faith. You must have infinite patience, often. And you must always have infinite faith.

With the goal a fixed point on your horizon, with your belief in the promises of your subconscious mind absolute, then you are ready to practice the techniques that will bring the idea to the point of reality.

So far, so good

Let me remind you, then, of the points we have made so far in this book. You must visualize, see a picture of yourself in possession of that which you want. You must use cards with that aim written on them as constant reminders to you; for the necessity to use repetition to make that picture take hold of your subconscious is one you must never forget.

Talk to your mirror; that is an open door from your conscious mind into your subconscious.

If your goal is distant, it may be wise to concentrate on each successive step in your progress, taking them up one by one. If you are the girl who wants to be an actress, she would concentrate first on her dramatic training; send for catalogues, ask advice, and having fixed on the school she thinks best fitted for her needs, set the task before her subconscious mind for accomplishment.

If you are the boy who wants to be a surgeon, your first aim, too, would be the selection of the proper school for your training. The whole point is to have a definite objective in mind; to believe; to go to work consciously to enlist the powers of your subconscious mind in bringing about that objective.

Even if your aim is not so distant your procedure is still the same. Decide on what you want, believe you will get it, see yourself in your mirror as possessing it, write it on your cards to remind you to keep the picture constant, and obey any instructions that come to you to bring about the end in view.

Believe; hold firm to your mental picture; obey. Nothing can keep you from success. For the subconscious mind never fails to obey any order given it clearly and emphatically by the conscious mind.

Chapter 12: GETTING AHEAD

SUCCESS IS A MATTER OF NEVER-CEASING APPLICATION.

You must work at it diligently - and forever.

Don't think that this method of thought control is a once-in-a-while practice for you to make use of only in times of sudden needs or desires. It is a habit of thinking, of working, of living.

You are teaching yourself an effective way of letting your mind, conscious and subconscious, control and direct you. It is a way of protecting yourself from the mistakes that too often wreck one's life. If you think that you can take it or leave it-you can't. When you get around to picking it up again, it won't be there. You will have lost it.

Nor must you yield to self-congratulation.

After you have had your first experience of success with this method, you will be tempted to feel that you've won your war. But there never is a final moment on your way toward success. With each attainment will come a new desire. And you will have to go to work on that in exactly the same manner that brought you to your first accomplished end. If you don't do this, you will find yourself slipping backward.

Life is fluid, never static. The time for the enjoyment of a sense of triumph never comes. Always you must be increasingly diligent to keep what you have won, to start on to the next goal.

Let's say you have attained a position that seems to you a cause for pride. There is sure to be somebody about who will want to take it from you.

Envy is always at work. If it becomes apparent that your hold on that position is weak, that you are not on your guard to keep it, the efforts on the part of others to push you off that rung on your ladder will increase. Unless they can see that you are on the alert to strengthen your position and to increase your hold, their countermoves will be immediate and too much for you. Never feel safe; never stop attacking.

The promise of the future

Forget the personal angle for the moment and look at this principle from the standpoint of patriotism. We are proud of our country: we believe it to be the finest in the world. The welfare of the individual is considered more conscientiously in the United States of America than almost anywhere else in the world.

We know, too, that our resources are still abundant, our future unpredictably great. Our advance in war potential is beyond our knowledge or imagination: in atomic and hydrogen bombs, radar, rocket guns, sea and aircraft. In the domestic field our use of metals' of plastics, of all sorts and kinds of materials opens into still unexplored regions. Our imaginations and our will-to-accomplish give promise of infinite future performance. Those of us who are alive fifty years hence will be looking on a world that will make this present one comparable to the Middle Ages.

And it is this will to advance that makes me feel safe about America.

A country that is contented is already a country that is beginning to decline. It is because I know that our laboratories and our scientists are at work on what might seem fantastic ideas that I feel safe.

One day our ships will be unsinkable; our machines will capture energy coming from the sun; there will even be recording devices to expose our unspoken thoughts. Science is pushing back the world's horizon. How? Imagination; and through imagination, the use of the subconscious.

Think big

It is claimed that man can produce materially anything that he can conceive mentally. We must grant that. When we stop to consider what is happening daily in the world around us, the idea loses its air of fantasy. And yet we know that we are only at the beginning.

When man fully comprehends the power of the mind and earnestly puts it to work, not only will he have dominion over this world but he will be reaching out toward the neighboring planets. That has begun already, has it not? Don't sit by and say "How wonderful!"

Get in and do your part! You, too, have that inner spark.

Use your mental equipment - use all of it. And by that use, keep it growing. Ask more and more of it all the time. And the fuel you feed that glowing ember, the fuel which fans it into a blaze is an *idea;* and another idea; and another idea.

You feed ideas into your conscious mind; you drive them down into your subconscious where they germinate, grow, and are given back to you in commands to act. Then, immediately, start another idea on that same route; a bigger idea, asking for more by way of growth, more by way of subsequent performance. Think big, imagine big, be big.

One man said to me that he was convinced that the people who failed had never started. "I plan," he said, "to start something new at least once a week. It may be nothing more than a gadget to ease my wife's work in the kitchen. It may be an experimental sales campaign. I may decide to open up new territory; or only to use a new slogan. I may do some unusual reading, breaking into a subject that is strange to me. But I keep my mind on the alert by asking something different of it all the time."

I doubt if it is necessary to spread one's self quite that thin: not a new subject every week - for a new idea on an old subject might accomplish considerably more. What you want is to dig deeper and deeper all the time into that well of knowledge and accomplishment you are visualizing for your next aim.

Whether you accept this man's idea of starting off on a new tack every week or decide to take a deeper bite into the activity upon which you are already engaged, the principle is the same. You are moving forward, not standing still.

Never stand still

This is important. There is an inertia in all of us that tempts us to contentment with an accomplishment. I say to myself, "I'm just where I wanted to go. I'll stay here a while and enjoy myself."

Don't! Train yourself to look ahead; train yourself in the possession of that valuable human asset, initiative. For initiative you must have if you intend to succeed in the undertaking you have set before yourself; toward which your alerted subconscious is prompting you to move. Without that constant stirring of ambition within you, that dissatisfaction with the present because your eyes are fixed so far ahead on the future, you will stop almost before you are started.

Inertia and inaction are static. You must continue to move or the backward slide will begin. You will never slip and slide upward without the constant drive and push of ambition. But you can easily slide backward without a single assist from your own mental faculties.

You must continually have new ideas; and you must put them to work.

The young man or woman who is content in the minor clerical job which he obtained when he first came out of school, that young person may still find himself in that same job when he reaches the age of sixty-five. Don't misunderstand me. I am not saying that he should not have taken the job, been glad of it. I am saying that he should do so well in it that he won't be allowed to remain there: he'll move on up in the organization. And unless he wants to stay there, he'd better begin on his first day and week in the job to be on the lookout for new ideas as to how he can do what he has to do better than it has ever been done before. If he makes himself more and more efficient, he is making himself more and more valuable to his employer.

Find a better way

Many organizations try to encourage their employees to take an imaginative part in the business. They put question boxes at convenient places for suggestions. They offer prizes for ideas that prove practicable. Use your mind; not just your conscious mind. Ask your subconscious mind to help you. Sometimes the idea that brings about a patentable device comes from a minor employee who thereby increases not only the firm's income but his own. Fortunes have been made by this means alone.

Remember: no matter how long a certain job has been done in just that certain way, there is always a better way.

If you are a clerk selling goods across the counter ideas must come to you constantly as to a better arrangement of your shelves, a better manner of displaying your goods, a better approach to your customers, a better attitude toward your superiors.

Keep your mind on the job: it will pay off.

But initiative takes more than a new idea to make you progress from your first job to the one higher up. You have to cultivate your own personality and charm: you have to assemble arguments to sell your idea. There are many avenues open for advancement to the young man or woman of ideas, and there are many different manners of approach. Let your subconscious guide you.

Initiative, new ideas and wisdom in the presenting of those ideas bring you as a by-product a most desirable asset: your interest in your work, your attention to it are automatically increased. And of course the more interest you take, the more attention to it you give, the better will you do that job.

We all know that we do best the things in which we are most interested.

Indeed, if you find nothing in your present job to interest you, no matter how diligently you search for such an attitude of mind, then you will have to concentrate your search on finding another sort of job. *For only absorbing interest will give you that momentum, that incentive that will make you succeed.*

A woman I knew was employed in a large mercantile organization. But her gift of imagination was so great that she very soon became assistant to the manager of the department to which she was assigned. In that capacity her ever-increasing initiative, her frequent suggestions for the betterment of the department brought her the largest Christmas bonus of any employee of that firm.

Keep your word

I know I'm going off on a bypath; I am supposed to be advising you as to how to use your own subconscious mind in your effort to achieve success. But I'd like to take time out just long enough to consider this matter of employer-employee relationship. After all it is a basic problem on which hangs many a young person's chance of success; so perhaps it is legitimate to look at it for a moment.

The personnel manager of a huge industrial plant told me the greatest fault he had to find with people was that they could not be depended on. They failed to keep their words; they were late to appointments; they were ever changing their minds.

If you know yourself to be such a person, look in your mirror and have it out with yourself. Give your subconscious mind the instructions that will correct these faults. Tell your conscious mind, look straight in your own eyes while you say it, that you want to be reliable; you want to keep your word, your appointments, fulfill all promises. Work at it. Establish that behavior pattern in yourself. If you do, you will have gone a long way toward attaining your aim.

Success comes almost unbidden to such a person.

Another employee problem of which this personnel manager complained was the attitude of "doing the firm a favor" by working.

Admitted, the firm needs the man's work, or it wouldn't hire him. But the man needs the job for which he is being paid or he wouldn't have applied for it, accepted it. So the firm is doing him a favor; it provides him not only with the opportunity to earn the salary which pays his living expenses but with a chance to attain skill, experience and wisdom that will carry him on and up in his search for success.

I'll even repeat that old truism: until a man has learned to take orders, he is not ready to give them. So the firm may even be training him for an executive position which will be his one day if his ability, personality, ambition and character warrant it. And all these requirements can be his if he asks his subconscious mind to work at the task of giving them to him.

Make friends - and be one

Incidentally, on your way to success learn to make friends. Not only do they help you on your way, they increase your joy of living. For life is more than a climb toward fame, accomplishment, success. Life is to be lived. And that's where friends count. And the making of friends is really a very simple matter. Just act on Emerson's advice: "The only way to have a friend is to be one."

I'm not advising you to make friends with everyone you meet. You will find yourself in tune with some people, out of tune with others. But as a rule you will find something admirable in most of your associates if you look for it. Don't let friction grow until you have made for yourself an active enemy. That is unwise as well as unpleasant. And you can usually turn ill will into good will. Here's a way to do it.

I knew an executive who had taken a violent dislike to one of his assistants who had criticized his procedure, and probably had not been too tactful in voicing that criticism. The assistant was able, but thereafter this executive never missed an opportunity to "show him up." The assistant knew this enmity was harmful to business, that it must end in the loss of his job unless he did something to end the friction.

So he consulted his mirror. "I know I started this feud," he told his image. "I was tactless and I'm sorry. The next time I'm with the boss I'm going to tell him so. It would be awkward if I came out with it openly, so I'll tell him so mentally."

Simple? Almost too simple. He repeated this process for several days. Then the time came when his subconscious prompted him to act. The two men happened to be alone in the elevator one morning and the assistant made an involuntary, friendly overture. "How's the boy?" he said with his usual infectious grin.

The response was immediate. The executive felt the friendliness in the other's attitude and involuntarily returned the other man's liking with liking.

You should never let enmity grow. The person with whom you have brushed unfriendly shoulders might not have continued to be offended unless you continued to be offensive. Be the first to make an advance, to offer an apology, to do some kindly act. You will seldom meet with rebuff. Think and believe that the other is basically a fine chap, and that is what he will turn out to be. We get back what we project, mentally. Our mirrors have been teaching us that.

Be courteous

Try this out; it's so simple, and easily proven. Do you use a bus frequently? Test the bus driver with a friendly "good morning." Or do you want to buy some article at a crowded counter? Don't grow impatient. Stand back and watch the harried clerk; send friendly thoughts out to her, sympathetic thoughts. She'll smile at you when your turn comes to be served and you will have taken some of the tension out of her face.

"As ye would that men should do to you, do ye even so to them," says the Bible. It is a workable principle and many successful men and women have adopted it, consciously or unconsciously.

I don't mean that you should calculate on a return for every kind or generous action. It doesn't work that way. But it does work if you count the law of averages. One person may have been too hurried and harried to show appreciation. But another may respond far more warmly than your tentative gesture requires. And anyway, your own mental state is kept at peace.

The person who feels kindly, deals generously, is rewarded. Not only is he or she happier but they get on better. Successful men and women know and practice this.

And it isn't a matter of apple-polishing. Trying to please the boss is both natural and wise. But it won't get you anywhere unless it's sincere. And the best way to insure that it is sincere is to go to work on your mirror: tell it to tell your subconscious mind to make it so. You have to work constantly on your own character. Watch for defects and correct them. It pays doubly: it brings you success, but it also brings you happiness along the way.

To be sure, promotion comes from the boss and it's a good idea to see to it that he is pleased with you. But the best way to please him is to do a superlative job. But you can be pleasant while you're doing it. And the people who work with you will be happier, kinder to you, more cooperative if they find such a spirit in you.

Forget about yourself

Think about this. Are you still in school? Which of your friends gets on best with all of you? You all like the friendly guy best, don't you? The self-centered boy - the one who sees nothing in school life to interest him except what he can get out of it for himself - he isn't your favorite companion, I'm sure. This is an angle that you must take into account while you are concentrating on success.

You, yourself, the person you are, must not be allowed to degenerate into a selfish, egotistical, pushing-other-people-aside sort of boy or girl. Talk this over with your mirror, too. Your subconscious will look after you. Your inner promptings will be kind, generous, unselfish if you tell your subconscious that you want them to be so.

The acts you are instructed to perform will never be mean. You can concentrate on success and still be a delight to your associates.

Take the initiative. Do something for the other fellow. And others - not he, necessarily - will do things for you. The world needs this spirit of give and take; help it along.

You know how it is with a dog. If he is petted, treated with kindness and affection, his tail wags and he tries to lick your face. But if anyone is cruel to him, scolds him, torments him, he strikes back. According to his breed and training, his growls may precede serious attack.

Human beings react in the same way. Some, more self-disciplined than others, are slow to show their resentment, but it is there. And anyone who has been the victim of thoughtlessness carries about a smoldering resentment that may bring unfortunate results to the careless perpetrator of the offense. Hurt feelings, controlled or not, always find some sort of outlet, either in action or in mental antagonism.

Lend a hand

Watch your behavior toward the people you meet even casually. Their reaction to you is important. If someone you know has done something admirable, tell him so. Sincere praise is always heartwarming. Too often our egos are stepped on by people and by life. We can do with a bit of inflation now and then.

We've all watched politicians build on this trait in human nature. Friendly people, to them, are favorable votes. They woo them in every possible way. They have a friendly word for the boy who delivers the newspaper, the chambermaid who serves them in any hotel room they occupy. They speak with hearty enthusiasm to the elevator boy or the doorman. This manner becomes a habit; and it is successful, as a rule, only to the extent that it is the result of a genuine liking for people.

Sincerity registers; so does insincerity.

I sat in the office of a store manager one day when an employee came in to thank him for advice he had given her. She had been offered a position in another city which would have brought her advancement, but she was timid and needed the push he had given her, the boost to her self-confidence.

When she left he said, "She'll make good: she has real ability. Do you know, one thing I like about my job is the chance it gives me to help a girl like that. I'm on the jump, as you can imagine. But somehow my people have a way of catching me when they have personal problems and, I assure you, I always have time for them. I suppose it flatters me; anyway, it makes me feel that I'm really worth something when my own store family turn to me in the crises in their lives."

That's the attitude I've been talking about. Climb, yes; be ambitious, by all means. Ask from yourself the very utmost your capabilities can deliver. But be human. Be sympathetic. Be helpful. It's the only way to keep happy as you pursue the course dictated by your ambition, plotted for you by your subconscious mind.

Be a wide-awake

"If you work for a man, for goodness' sake work for him," said Elbert

Hubbard. Which, of course, is in line with all that we have been saying about having a sincere interest in the work you are doing. This lack of interest is more widespread than you'd think; and it is found in the worker who never gets promoted. Not only are such men and women uninterested in their own jobs, they are indifferent to everything outside the jobs. They don't read the newspapers; except, perhaps, for sporting events. They can't answer the simplest questions about the towns or cities in which they live: population, industries, local government, cultural advantages.

I made a wager with the executive of a large concern, a man whose name was in the newspapers almost daily, for his interests and affiliations were widespread. I bet him that I could find at least twenty people in his organization who did not know him by name. He thought I was crazy and was considerably nettled when I won the bet.

Curiosity prompted me to check with comparable organizations. The result was always the same. Few employees knew or cared who the men were who owned and ran the business which paid them their salaries. The name and personality of the person next higher up was important. The amount in the weekly or monthly pay envelope was important. But anything other than the immediate facts that touched their personal relationship was of no interest.

This is not a recommended policy for the young person who means to go forward from where he stands. Whether the job you hold is your first job, or one in which you've been resting securely and indifferently for a matter of months or years, wake up! If your world is small, widen it.

Be interested in your own job, in the jobs of all the others in the organization, from the bottom to the top. Find out about them. Fit yourself to be either the errand boy of the confidential adviser to the president or the secretary who takes his dictation.

Grow. Push your roots deep and let your branches spread. Know the heads of the various departments: not only their duties but their personalities. Go about with a mind wide open and interested in every phase of every operation in the concern that employs you.

Be curious. Ask questions. For one thing, it is only that kind of mind and attack that receives the stimulus of new ideas. The more you know about the details of the workings of an organization, the more you will perceive its flaws, the more ideas for the improvement of its machinery will you be able to offer for the consideration of those above you.

Easy does it

This is where caution is necessary. Remember the sensitive egos with which you are surrounded. The young person who goes about telling everybody about him how he could improve his way of doing things isn't going to endear himself to his co-workers.

Know all you can; grow, mentally. But be slow to offer your suggestions.

Confine all your efforts in the beginning to widening and smoothing and meshing your own groove. Opportunities to help the other fellow do the same in his particular spot will come to you; as he feels in you disinterested helpfulness, he will ask.

Say, for example, that you are ready to move into the job next above the one you are in. But it's occupied. You don't want to push him out; you want to push him up. So go to work on that. Study the job next above him; help him to fit himself for it. You can stir his thinking, stimulate his ambition without giving offense if he believes in your friendliness. Didn't I say people are important? And your ability to get on with people will be one of the most important tools in your upward journey.

Books are tools

"Man is heir to the wisdom of the ages found within the covers of great books," remarked a very wise man. What about it? Do you know and use that kind of wisdom? You'd better. Of all your tools, it is the most valuable.

A college education has taught you nothing unless it has led you to seek and find the truths that lie in the works of the scholars of past generations. I am appalled, dismayed, astonished, horrified, at the degeneracy that has come to the reading habits of the American youth; yes, and to American adults as well. Radios, television, magazine capsule reading matter aren't to be blamed; they aren't cause but effect. They give us in brief that which we are too lazy-minded to take at leisure.

Enjoyment beyond the comprehension of the non-reader comes from books. Knowledge otherwise altogether missed comes from books. And in books you will often come upon your most important ideas for advancement. All the accomplishments of civilization are yours; you can go on from there instead of cutting your own path through the underbrush, only to arrive at an open space already occupied. The tales of inventors who fritter away years on inventions already patented are well known.

Know your job. Know the people with whom you come in contact. Know the opportunities of the community in which you live. And know what books have to give you. These are your tools; these bring growth; these, you may be sure, will be the prompters of your subconscious. And from all these sources will come the ideas which are the fuel you must feed your conscious mind in order to promote that combustion action by which the subconscious drives you on.

Where joy is found

I will digress again to remind you to get joy as well as progressive successful accomplishments out of life. If it isn't fun as you go along, it won't be fun when you get there. So don't confine your reading to search for information in your own field.

Joy comes of following bypaths. If the world of poetry is strange to you, explore it. If you've neglected history and biography, you'll find much there to interest you.

For here is another truism: *knowledge is power.* Don't skip that sentence just because you've heard it so often.

Knowledge *is* power. And you will find your bits of out-of-the-usual information resulting from this off-track reading will contribute unexpectedly, even spectacularly to your growing brain power. Your thinking will be stimulated, your efforts accelerated. The subconscious mind works better for an informed, thinking, conscious mind.

Chapter 13: THE WANDERING MIND

EVERY STUDENT OF PSYCHOLOGY - EVEN THE AMATEUR

INQUIRER - is familiar with the phenomenon of association of ideas.

One idea seems to link itself to another without your volition. You can find no reason for that inconsequent second idea: yet there it is. And it may be the more important of the two.

An automobile overturned at the side of the road suggests at once the unpleasant details of an accident. Your mind wanders from there to the possible uses of scrap metal and from there to boy scouts. This may reverse your progress and you will wonder if that wreck was the result of young speedsters and you are led to meditate on the problems of juvenile delinquency.

This trick of the mind to follow a zigzag trail may prove of value to you. If you are practicing obedience to subconscious promptings, there may be meaning in these ideas. If you are a social worker some practical theory about dealing with the driving habits of the young may develop from that overturned automobile. It is wise to follow through those straying ideas; you can't be sure where you are being led by this chain thinking.

How ideas grow

Suppose you are walking in the woods and you pick up a nut. You begin to wonder idly about the occupation of nut-growing. What about soil and labor? How would you compete with nuts already well established in their marketing programs. Packaging? That is the most important single item in a sales campaign.

But you're in the mercantile business; and here you are with a packaging idea that may make you a fortune. And all of it, the whole full-grown plan, came from the nut picked up in a stroll through the woods.

This is the way ideas grow; this is the reason for encouraging your mind in its seeming woolgathering. You may be led in a direction that ends in a dead end. Then you'll discard the whole product.

Dealers may not go along with your packaging idea. Or the public may not find the eye appeal all that you thought it. But - and this is my point - if your idea has been reached as a result of subconscious prompting, it won't fail. Ideas must be encouraged.

I remember when our western apples were selling by the wagonload and didn't pay for the labor of picking. Then one Pacific Northwest apple grower had a packaging idea. His apples were sorted, the finest wrapped in paper labeled EXCLUSIVES. Those apples sold for ten cents apiece and paid for the labor and shipping charges of the entire crop. The whole apple-growing industry was affected. Now it is not unusual for a box of a dozen spectacularly wrapped apples to sell for two dollars. When they couldn't improve the product, they stepped up the eye appeal.

Learn to package yourself

Consider this matter of packaging with reference to yourself. Don't ask your subconscious to do all the work. Let your conscious mind give it all the help it can. It's your conscious mind that you are at pains to train and educate: that will give your subconscious mind all the more to work with. Think of your subconscious mind as the employer; of your conscious mind as the eager employee.

All right; what about your own appearance? Indeed, it may well be your subconscious mind that is prompting you to this inquiry. One never knows whence in this matter of ideas.

Do you have eye appeal? What about your clothes, your bearing, the expression of your face? Do they break down the reserves of the one you wish to impress? And here again, a word of caution.

There is such a thing as eye appeal that works against you instead of for you. A spectacular appearance may be exactly the wrong approach. You will need a knowledge of the mental slant of the person with whom you have to deal in order to judge as to your own best attack. But it is usually wise to lean toward conservatism. The unobtrusive but "right" appearance will go farther as a rule than the "arresting."

Study yourself. Know your own personality. Choose the colors and designs that suit you; but let your appearance, in so far as is possible, express the real and essential "you." Let your clothes, bearing and facial expression say to the one you meet exactly what you are.

This isn't so simple as it sounds. You want to stand out from the crowd without being obtrusive. You want to please without arousing competition. When you have found the way to dress that is *your* way, when your body and your mind say the same thing, then you have an unbeatable combination.

You may think I am overemphasizing an unimportant point. I'm not. Too often accomplishment depends on first impressions. Life has a way of accelerating at the important moments. A decision has to be made in a hurry, and it is vital that it be in your favor.

Who gets the attention?

Look around you. Watch the behavior of crowds. Isn't it the well-dressed man with the pleasant manner who gets preferred treatment? Make an excuse to sit in the office of some important business executive. Watch the procedure. Who gets in to see the great man - the next in line? Not always. It may well be the well-groomed, charming fellow who goes straight to the secretary's desk to remind her of his appointment.

Try to get the newspaper reporter who covers the police station and jail to let you trail him about for a day. You'll learn things. The tramp goes straight into a cell but the poised offender, well dressed and sure of himself, gets to sit in the captain's chair while he telephones his lawyer. He looks important; he might be "somebody." Unfair? Of course. But that's the way things are: these men have to make snap judgments and they have nothing to guide them but appearances.

Learn to take advantage of that tendency which is in every one of us to give more attention to the person who looks like "someone" than to the one who doesn't. And the best way to look like someone important is to think that you are. Dress yourself attractively and then forget about your looks. Concentrate on your mental attitude; think success thoughts; feel an outgoing interest in whatever you see, whomever you meet. Know that the other fellow is going to like you, be interested in you just as you are in him. It will work.

A young man on the sales force of a big distributing agency, as the result of fortunate circumstances, was given the assignment of closing a deal with a very wealthy man, a man who always bought the most expensive cars. Of course he was scared: this was his first big chance to prove his worth, his ability.

"Not only did I go home and take a shower," he told me, "but I changed all my clothes. I went to a barbershop and had a shampoo and the first manicure of my life. It'll be the last one, too: it made me feel like a sissy. Anyway, it took my mind off my sales problem."

"Did you sell the car?" I asked.

"Sure," he grinned. "It was sold before I even met the man. I felt as if I could lick my weight in wildcats; so what chance had a mere tycoon?"

Naturally he'd been getting his mind ready while he showered and changed his clothes. He'd been building up inner power while he was in the barber chair. He'd given his subconscious orders and his subconscious was delivering. His conscious mind was given the task of selling a car; it in turn told the subconscious mind to see to the matter. He'd been throwing around himself the aura of success. His imagination had been at work producing in him a personal magnetism that could not fail.

Many years ago I was getting a story from the chief of a metropolitan fire department. The man seemed to fear nothing; his associates believed he had a charmed life. I asked him about that.

"I don't know as you'd call it 'charmed,'" he said. "Maybe I am a sort of fatalist. I've always believed I couldn't be killed as long as I'm chief. When I go into a place I always throw a white circle around myself and nothing can get inside that circle. It's a trick I learned from the Indians who lived near us when I was a kid. Probably that's the worst kind of superstition but that circle has saved my life more times than I like to think about."

He lived out his life as chief, and he died of natural causes in his seventies.

Remember the time Babe Ruth "called his shot"? Here was a man who had become so confident of his ability to do a certain thing that, just once, he wanted to *predict* that he would do it: hit a home run and even point to the place in the stands where the ball would go. Of course, if you know baseball you know that that's impossible, even for a Ruth. But the Babe's subconscious mind prompted him, he pointed to the stands in center field, and wham! There was the ball sailing into the stands just where he had pointed. He had obeyed that impulse from his subconscious - and it worked.

My fire-chief friend is not the only man of my acquaintance who has put that white circle of safety around himself. Soldiers in war have done it and come through. Belief has a way of paying off.

Protect your emotions

But if we are to trust our own emotional natures, refusing to be governed by reason alone, we have to perform another task. We must realize that the vibrations set up by others affect us much more than we realize. Often we will find ourselves taking on the characteristics of those with whom we more or less constantly associate.

Husband and wife, after long years of close and sympathetic living together, come to resemble each other in personality as well as in mind. A baby, almost from birth, takes on the emotional characteristics of those who care for it. It becomes susceptible to the fears, likes and dislikes of its mother or nurse. Frequently these emotional qualities persist with it through life.

That, obviously, is the basis for the psychiatrist's efforts to dig back into the past of an emotionally disturbed patient. He wants to find the childhood experience which has caused the dislocation he perceives in the adult. We see a personality shift in a child when he is of an age to go to school. And he alters his emotional pattern with each successive classroom teacher. We are all far more susceptible than we realize to the emotional rest or unrest of our associates.

Aren't you aware of the contrast in atmosphere between one home and another? Usually it is the mother that sets the pattern though the father may bring into a peaceful daytime atmosphere a chaotic evening one.

An extremely nervous person in a position of authority can put his whole staff on edge. You are familiar with the saying that an organization is only the extended shadow of the man who heads it.

When you're choosing your first job, it might be well to take this into account. If possible, go to work for the kind of person with whom you can feel "easy." It will increase your efficiency and your happiness.

It is not unusual for an employer to discover that a single member of his staff is stirring up unrest in the entire body. A strong negative personality, out of tune with the ideas of the management, can extend its destructive vibrations and do great damage, just as one rotten apple in a box will, unless quickly discovered and removed, cause all the others to rot.

You've seen a person yawning in a waiting room or bus start everybody yawning. And we're familiar with the contagion of laughter or tears. Few of us realize how much our own emotional vibrations affect others and how much we are affected by theirs.

How others affect you

If you would remain a positive type, avoid association with anyone of a negative or pessimistic slant of mind. Many clergymen and personnel counselors become the victims of prolonged association with people who come to them only to tell their troubles. The impact of the steady stream of woe and sorrow vibrations eventually reverses their own positive, wholesome personalities.

If you think I am overemphasizing this danger, watch your own reactions to people and surroundings. You are immediately at ease or you are unreasonably and unreasoningly disturbed. The person whose office or home you have entered is either a cold or a warm personality. You will even read hints of this in the arrangement of furniture, the choice of pictures on the wall, the color scheme of the curtains and upholstery. The whole room vibrates to the one who lives there and reflects the personality.

Why do you think theater people make such a point of the setting for a play? The producer wants to win from the audience, even before a word is said on the stage, a response to the mood which the playwright has created, in which his story must move. If the stage designer's mental reaction to the play has clashed with the author's intention, the audience will receive a discordant vibration. Indeed, the play may well fail.

Does all this discussion of favorable and unfavorable vibrations alarm you? It well may. Everything for you will depend on whether you are the "leader" or the "follower" type of person. And the followers are more numerous than the leaders. If you are to get anywhere in life - and I assume you are or you wouldn't be reading this book - you will have to join the "leader" fraternity.

So long as you evade responsibilities, are afraid of making decisions, want to be told what to do, are afraid to step out alone, just so long you will be out of step with your destiny.

Tackle your problems

You are confronted with a problem: tackle it. The longer you postpone it, the more fearful you will grow as to your ability to solve it. Force yourself to make decisions. When you do not decide, when you vacillate, you fail to act. And a failure to act invites failure.

Once a decision is made - you will learn this by experience - the troubles begin to disappear. You may not have made the wisest decision, but even so you will gain more by action than by inaction. You will feel an accession of strength. Your morale will rise. Fear of doing the wrong thing actually attracts the wrong thing.

Decide. Act. Whether you've made a mistake or not the chances are that your difficulties will fade into thin air. All great men are men of quick decisions, because they are men of intuition. Learn to be quick in your decisions and audacious in your actions.

I make no claim to being a faith healer. But anybody who has studied the powers of the mind knows the effect of emotionalized thinking upon the condition of the body. We all admit the power of suggestion in bringing on disease, as well as in curing it.

Some faith healing movements effect their cures by denying that the disease exists, and thousands attest to the validity of this method. Others do not deny the existence of disease, but they meet it by affirmation: they insist that they are well and happy and getting better every day. This appears to work, too. But in all cases, as I have said repeatedly, *it is the individual's belief* that determines the success of the method of cure. Just how far suggestion can be used to cure disease or physical disability is still a matter of controversy. But the fact remains that there are thousands in our country alone who believe that the cure of their ailments has come as a result of mental healing.

Emotional ailments

Emotions such as hate, fear, worry lead to physical ills, even to fatal diseases. *Life* magazine published an article on *Psychosomatic Medicine* - by the term *psychosomatic* we mean bodily ailments brought on by the emotions - which declared that 40 percent of all army disabilities brought on by the war had originated from psychosomatic causes.

The article pointed out that many cases of hay fever, bronchial asthma, heart disease, high blood pressure, rheumatic disease, arthritis, the common cold, and various skin conditions such as warts, hives and allergic reactions were caused by emotional upsets directly or by physical disturbances in which the emotions were an aggravating factor. The treatment consisted in locating the emotional disturbance and trying to cure it.

Because of the experiments of the psychiatrists during the war the whole subject of medical and mental treatment of disease is undergoing complete revision.

Cure yourself

However those who understand the science of psycho-therapeutics are fairly agreed that a cure does not come through treatment on the part of the healer nearly so much as it does from the patient himself. In other words, the suggestion, no matter in what form it is given by the healer (whether in accordance with the principles of psychotherapeutics or with some special religious belief) must be transmitted by the patient himself to his own subconscious mind if it is to become effective. If the patient refuses to believe in the suggestions of the healer, the cure will not take place. Healer and patient have to be *en rapport* to get results.

It is my belief that any person who possesses an understanding of the use of the power of suggestion can get results without the aid of a healer, provided he is strong and constant in his convictions and suggestions. The techniques we have been studying - cards, mirror, affirmation, repetition - can be used to great advantage.

With each chapter we come full circle back to our premise: the attainment of our desires, even to the healing of our bodies, comes of thinking, believing, wholeheartedly and over a length of time.

Our own minds make our destiny.

Chapter 14: MASTER OF YOURSELF

REMEMBER: *belief is a power working destructively as well as constructively.*

If you are a believer, don't open a passage from your subconscious mind to the subconscious mind of an unbeliever. His unbelief may be stronger than your belief and able to destroy the results after which you are striving. That is one reason why I warn you continually against talking to others about your excursions into the realm of thought power.

There is magic in believing. Believe that it will work and it will. But another's disbelief may hamper or even destroy the results of your efforts.

Whether it be mind - as we understand the general usage of the Word - or electrical vibrations of some kind, the results are startling. The effects of the phenomena with which we are dealing embrace and pervade everything. For all practical purposes we may consider the subconscious mind of anyone person - yours or mine - as a very small part of a great whole, extending to and embracing everything.

Belief, as I keep repeating, is essential. And belief comes often as the result of successful experimentation.

Belief grows as you use it; its power grows in proportion to the increasing degree of your faith. You have nothing to lose and everything to gain, so give yourself to a conscientious study of this theory, to a trial-and-error investigation of its astounding principles.

Don't go through life doubting everything; skeptics always sit on the sidelines. It is the believer that gets into the game; and while he may lose, he also has the only chance to win. And isn't that preferable to watching someone else play for the important stakes of life? Dare to make mistakes; it is one way to find truth.

A horticulturist once advised me: "Don't be afraid to prune; if you spoil your roses for this year, they will be the better for it next year." If your aim in life is to find truth, to make the most of yourself, to be a useful and productive member of society, you owe it to yourself to give these principles of thought power a thorough workout.

Try them and try them again, until you are thoroughly convinced of their workability, until you know that for you they are successful.

Never neglect your gift

And when you are convinced, never let the power lie unused. I say now as I have said before: you can lose the gift if you neglect it. Be a conscientious user of all the techniques I have indicated. I wouldn't offer them to you if they were merely unproved theory. They have worked for me; they have, to my certain knowledge, worked for hundreds of other people.

Let me recapitulate.

Hold up before your own eyes and mind an image of the kind of person you mean to be, the aim which you have set your heart on accomplishing. Make a picture: see yourself in the act, see the place in life to which you aspire and yourself as occupying that place. Make this picture distinct in every detail; no blurred edges. Make it so definite that it flashes before your mind's eyes without any conscious effort on your part to bring it up.

Add to that definite picture the rite of repetition.

Reduce your ambition to the simplest possible phrases and repeat them to yourself until they become as familiar, as ritualistic as the refrain of a popular song. Use your cards as reminders to keep this repetition constant. These reminders are important; you may think you will not need them but you do. Other events crowd into your mind for attention. But beneath all daily happenings you must keep up your concentration on your duty to keep your conscious mind at work, prompting your subconscious mind into active participation.

Don't neglect the use of your mirror as a means of talking to yourself, of transmitting through your conscious mind your need of your subconscious.

Look yourself in the eyes: see what you are, and see what you want to be. You know how often you look directly into the eyes of your friends, or into your father's or mother's eyes when you want to reassure yourself as to the depth of meaning; as to how seriously you must take what they are saying. As you stare into your own eyes, tell yourself that you believe: watch your eyes until they answer and assure you that they, also, believe. "Ask and ye shall receive: seek and ye shall find." That is not only Biblical, that is common sense.

But the uses of the subconscious mind need not be confined to acting as director in the accomplishment of your expressed ambition. You can use it as director of your unformed opinions and duties.

When you are uncertain, undecided, call upon the subconscious to bring clarity to your thinking, guidance to your actions. It is possible, as the last conscious act of your mind before going to sleep, to commit to the subconscious the problem about which you are in such confusion. Put before it all your arguments for and against. Then sleep peacefully.

More often than not when you awake in the morning your decision will be made, all your reasons for that decision neatly arrayed in your conscious mind. And if, for some reason, the subconscious is not ready with the decision in the morning, you will receive it in a vivid flash that is an unmistakable subconscious message either during the day or at some future time. But you will be told; that is beyond question or doubt. You need not give the matter another moment of anxiety.

White magic

I've talked enough, perhaps, about charms and amulets, discs and talismans. "Superstition" is the easy way in which we dismiss the whole array. But what does that word "superstition" mean? It is something which another person believes and you do not; isn't that about all you can say of it?

An actor believes that he will forget his lines unless he wears a certain charm around his neck or carries a "lucky" silver dollar in his pocket. He forgets his charm and he forgets his lines. He thinks it was the charm that defeated him: I think it was his belief in the charm. What difference? The result was the same.

We know that voodoo practitioners do have the power of life or death over their victims - if the victim believes firmly enough in that power. Such a man has only to be notified of his impending fate and he sickens and dies. Usually no power can save him. That is black magic.

Then there is white magic. What I am dealing with is white magic: I am striving to make *you* believe.

If you believe, you may be what you wish; you may go where you wish. The power which that believing, that wishing, will develop will take you where you want to go.

Set yourself a goal; never weaken or waver and you will reach that goal.

The word "waver" is important. It is so easy to lose faith, to lose hope; then regain them; then lose them. "Blowing hot and cold," our parents used to call that state of mind. That is the simplest way for you to defeat yourself. Go to work on your conscious mind; don't permit yourself to waver. Your cards will prompt you to this necessity. Make a routine of your talks with yourself in the mirror. Time these consultations and don't miss one of them.

It is more important, my girl, than setting your hair or cold-creaming your face before going to bed.

It is vastly more important, young man, than those setting-up exercises with which you greet the day.

Look yourself in the eye and tell yourself that you believe. How many magazine stories have you read that use, as a central theme, the loss of faith which brings almost tragedy and deep sorrow until the circumstances are explained.

Your mind is yourself

A story trick? Not at all: a psychological truth.

Faith, belief - even though facts seem to point to betrayal - is an essential to your soul life. And if it is important to have faith in another, why is it not important to have faith in yourself? For your mind *is* yourself.

So look yourself in the eye and assure yourself that you believe. Keep at it until you feel a surge of belief cleaning out all your doubts. Keep this up. Don't permit yourself to lose faith: you may hamper the workings of your subconscious just when it needs the power which comes to it only from your faith.

Another caution: keep working after you have arrived. Too many people let down their guard, sit back happily, relax. "This is wonderful," they say. "Now I can enjoy myself."

It isn't wonderful and you can't enjoy yourself; that is, no more than you have been enjoying yourself all along the way. How many novelists are known as "one-book" men or women? Why? They put it all into that first great product; then they begin to coast. They have "arrived." You've heard me say it before, now I'm saying it again. You *never* arrive.

The future is always beckoning, more shining, more difficult of achievement than the past. Look about you: notice the people of your acquaintance who are known in the community for just one notable deed; examine their subsequent behavior. They aren't trying to go ahead, only to stand still. So, of course, they are slipping backward.

So when you have reached your goal, *look ahead.* You've succeeded, but the only power on earth that can keep that success for you, make it permanent, is your subconscious.

You must continue to consult it, give it your orders, keep it marching. Cooperate with your subconscious always; believe in it; obey its promptings. Keep in touch. Talk to it through your mirror. Or has that mirror habit become so fixed in you by the time you have arrived at your first goal that you no longer need my cautioning? If so, you are among the fortunate of the earth. You will never slip, never go backward but always forward. The poet, Longfellow, whose gift it was to state the obvious in unforgettable terms, said it all in his poem *Excelsior!* Read it.

Keep at it - the day will come

I know it is difficult for the average person to accept these conclusions, to convince himself of the necessity for this constant experimenting on himself. In fact, the only way for you to convince yourself or others that you are living on a plane above the "average person" is for you to continue this mirror habit, this card habit, this habit of consulting and trusting to your subconscious.

It takes effort to lift our minds out of the region of influence exerted by the mass mind of the average thinking. Too long have we accepted the generally admitted conclusion that life is lived on the physical plane; that we are at the mercy of chance, that others and not ourselves will determine our destinies. The universality of this belief is what gives it power. That is the reason your own use of your own mental forces takes such constant and persistent effort.

You're bucking - well, perhaps not an avalanche - but a huge, sluggish mud bank.

So, if you are a young person deeply concerned with making something of yourself, achieving for yourself a really distinguished future, evade this inertia of general, mass disbelief by keeping your own beliefs secret; by exercising continuously the active powers of your subconscious mind, giving it the continuous stimulus you furnish through your promptings to your conscious mind.

This is important; indeed, it may prove vital. The materialist is so sure that nothing spiritual exists that you only weaken your own faith when you talk with him. Let him live on that plane if he likes; you accept the great, opening realm of the spirit in which to dwell.

And presently only the image you create in your mind will have reality to you. You will be as impervious to the disbelief of the cynic as he is to your belief.

Happiness is a state of mind

Happiness, sought by the many and found by the few, is a matter entirely within your own powers of achievement. Your environment, the everyday happenings of your life have absolutely no effect on your capacity for happiness. Nothing outside yourself can affect you unless you permit its image to enter your consciousness.

Stand guard over your mind. Don't let anything in that you do not want there. Happiness is independent of position, wealth, material possessions. It is a state of mind which you yourself have the power to control, because you are the guardian of your own thinking.

If your subconscious mind is not opened up to unhappiness by the images furnished by your conscious mind, you will feel no unhappiness. You can be as happy as you like.

A child's imagination

When you were a child did you compare the surroundings you found in your own home with those of your playmates who might be more fortunate (or unfortunate) than you? Of course you didn't. You liked to play with the children who had more to offer than others in the way of ideas, imagination, play suggestions. It is more than likely that those children came from the less privileged homes rather than from the stultifying atmosphere of the more privileged.

Things stifle; they always have. And happiness, overpowering happiness comes to a child only by way of his imagination. To him a teacher who is understanding is beloved and he would give her his most treasured possessions, a seashell that sings in your ear or a stone of unusual coloring when it is wet.

But the teacher who is unjust (childhood's criterion for love or hatred) becomes the object of all his ingenuity in the art of persecution. He is dealing with the "wicked one," and you cannot convince him that his misbehavior is "wrong."

The values of childhood are not material but mental. His standard is more likely to conform to Emerson's true and beautiful than to the Puritan's rigid "righteousness" and "sin."

It would be well if we carried over into adulthood something of the perceptiveness of the child to spiritual values. Keep your happiness a matter between your conscious and your subconscious minds.

Your parents and you

I am not saying that you may not enjoy material possessions.

Does another girl have prettier clothes than you? Tell your conscious mind to prompt your subconscious mind to help you in achieving them for yourself. This is feasible so long as you do not let the ugly quality of envy cloud your mental processes.

Would you like to see your family living in a more commodious and beautiful home? It is legitimate to put your subconscious to work in helping you achieve that aim. But keep your happiness while the process is going on. That is, keep your aim clear while you are working for that more beautiful house, but don't confuse your wish for its possession with any unkind thoughts of the person who has already the things you want.

Say you are a boy whose father is so immersed in his business or in his own external activities that he is unaware of the needs of a growing boy for the companionship and affection that the father has, in reality, for his son but does not permit expression in acts and words.

You, that boy, can go to work on that. By your picturing, by your mental concentration, your subconscious mind can reach your father's subconscious mind as no words could ever do. You can tell him what you need from him, and his subconscious mind will warn him of your need and prompt him to fill that need.

In your working before your mirror, *see* your father in the acts you want from him; asking you to go fishing with him or to a ball game; or just walking and talking with you; whatever it is that you are missing from his behavior. See it in your mirror; believe it; and it will come.

"Consider," said that great philosopher, Marcus Aurelius Antoninus, "that everything is opinion, and opinion is in thy power. Take away then, when thou choosest, thy opinion, and like a mariner, who had doubled the promontory, thou wilt find calm, everything stable, and a waveless bay."

You can prove this for yourself. When something has disturbed you, examine your mental attitude. Are you disappointed? That is an emotional reaction, isn't it? Meet it and fight it mentally. Drive it out of your conscious. Replace it with other and calmer thoughts. Don't let it reach your subconscious. Because if you permit it to lodge there, it will make you keep your unhappiness, even wallow in it. If you compel yourself to stop thinking about it, presently you will find that you are no longer emotional about it.

Be the boss of your own habits of thought; guard and protect your subconscious from unwanted emotions, whether of unhappiness, hatred, envy, any forms of meanness. If you wish, you can become unconquerable.

Emerson said: "What is the hardest task in the world? To think."

That is obvious, isn't it? Try to realize how completely you are the victim of mass thinking. Where do you get your ideas? Are they original, the result of your own mental processes? I doubt it. Someone has told you something; you've read a newspaper item or a magazine article. You accept these suggestions without argument, without reasoning about them, asking yourself what degree of truth is back of them.

If the magazine article has been written by a person obviously involved, emotionally, in his subject matter, you can't trust him to have given an unbiased view. If the person who has told you something or other about some other person is a notorious gossip who relishes the bit of scandal she is passing on, don't be too willing to believe the truth of what she has said. Think, use your best judgment, evaluate; then decide.

Live your own life

If you want to get anywhere in the world, accomplish anything of worth, be happy, like living with yourself, make up your mind to live your own life with your own mind.

Learn to think. Many times the entire course of a man's life has been changed by a single thought. It has come to him in a flash out of his subconscious and has become a mighty power, sometimes altering the whole current of human events. History has been made by strong-minded, resolute-willed individuals who, steadfastly holding to their inner convictions, have been able to inspire and lead others. Such men and women, in the face of tremendous and determined opposition, have literally created out of nothing great businesses, huge empires, new worlds.

Read history. If you need further convincing of the power of thought, read the lives of the great men of history. See how steadfastly these leaders of our universe have held to a fixed purpose, a dream, an ideal. They have literally thought and believed their way to success.

And they have no monopoly on thought power. You have it; I have it; so has everyone. All anyone needs to do is to use it. You will become the person your imagination pictures you.

By the constant, determined use of your mental powers you will bring into your life new elements. Your dominant thought will create within and attract from without.

Positive, creative thought leads to action and to ultimate realization. Power, real power is in thought. The action to which your thinking prompts you is the means to the end but not the guiding force. Remember always: Whatever man can conceive mentally, he can bring into materialization." Health, wealth, happiness, usefulness must follow if the proper mental pictures are created. But, I must continue to remind and caution, *those pictures must be maintained; for the law of cause and effect is unchangeable.*

Use your power

"Know thyself." Know your power.

Believe in yourself; and believe in the undefeatable power of your mind to give you what you ask of it.

Read and reread this book; practice and continue to practice the routines you have been taught here. Let them become a part of your daily life, as inevitable as the movements of going to bed at night, of getting up in the morning, of eating and sleeping and exercising, of doing your various tasks.

Let the promptings of your cards, the picturing before your conscious mind, the interviews with your mirror have their place in that routine, so fixed by habit that there is no more likelihood of your forgetting them than there is of your neglecting to comb your hair or wash your face. This isn't something to be put on and off like a coat that you wear only when you need its protection against the weather.

Mind power is something you need every moment of every day, waking or sleeping. And mind power becomes weak like the unused muscles of your body if you neglect the exercises that keep it in trim.

If you keep to these exercises, you won't have to *try* to believe, you *will* believe. And believing, you will win for yourself the rewards of believing.

There is genuine creative magic in believing, *when you believe.*

Belief will supply the power that will enable you to succeed in everything that you undertake, when you are in the habit of seeking guidance from your subconscious. Follow through with the techniques of applying your mental faculties to the desired end.

Back your belief with a resolute will and you will be unconquerable, master of circumstances and - far more important - master of yourself.

Recommended Readings

- Siddhartha, Hermann Hesse, www.bnpublishing.net

- TNT: It Rocks the Earth, Claude M. Bristol, www.bnpublishing.net

- The Anatomy of Success, Nicolas Darvas, www.bnpublishing.net

- The Dale Carnegie Course on Effective Speaking, Personality Development, and the Art of How to Win Friends & Influence People, Dale Carnegie, www.bnpublishing.net

- The Law of Success In Sixteen Lessons by Napoleon Hill (Complete, Unabridged), Napoleon Hill, www.bnpublishing.net

- It Works, R. H. Jarrett, www.bnpublishing.net

- The Art of Public Speaking (Audio CD), Dale Carnegie, wwww.bnpublishing.net

- The Success System That Never Fails (Audio CD), W. Clement Stone, www.bnpublishing.net

BN Publishing

Improving People's Life

www.bnpublishing.net

BN Publishing

Improving People's Life

www.bnpublishing.net

Breinigsville, PA USA
06 September 2010
244927BV00003B/25/P